GCSE Business and Communication Systems
The Workbook

This book is for anyone doing **GCSE Business and Communication Systems** or **GCSE Business Communications**.

It's full of **tricky questions**... each one designed to make you **sweat** — because that's the only way you'll get any **better**.

It's also got some daft bits in to try and make the whole experience at least vaguely entertaining for you.

What CGP is all about

Our sole aim here at CGP is to produce the highest quality books — carefully written, immaculately presented and dangerously close to being funny.

Then we work our socks off to get them out to you — at the cheapest possible prices.

Contents

Section One — Business Essentials
Why Businesses Exist 1
Enterprise 2
Business Ownership Structures 3
Customers 4
Stakeholders 5
Measuring Business Success 6
Starting a New Business 7
Succeeding as a New Start-Up 8
Businesses and the Law 9

Section Two — Marketing and Finance
Marketing and Market Research 10
Analysing the Market 11
Prices, Revenue, Costs and Profit 12
Finance and Cash Flow 13
The Economic Environment 14

Section Three — Organisation & Administration
Organisational Structure 15
Administration in Business 16
Routine & Non-Routine Tasks 17
Planning 18
Efficient Use of Resources 19
Office Layout 20

Section Four — Human Resources
Patterns of Work 21
Recruitment — Job Analysis 22
Recruitment — The Selection Process 23
Employment Law 24
Staff Training 25
Financial Rewards 26
Modern Working Practices 28
Health and Safety at Work 29

Section Five — Businesses and Data
Data Processing Systems 30
Computers and Input Devices 31
More Input Devices 32
Data Storage 33
Data Storage and Back-Up 34
Output Devices — Printers 35
More Output Devices 36
Keeping Data Secure 37
Data Protection and the Law 38

Section Six — Communication

Purposes of Communication 39
Internal and External Communication 40
Barriers to Communication 41
Written Communication — Letters 42
Internal Written Communication 43
More Written Communication 44
Electronic Communication 45
Face-to-Face Meetings 47
Other Oral Communication 48
Visual Communication 49
Changing a Communication System 50

Section Seven — Businesses and the Web

How Businesses Use the Internet 51
Business Websites — Benefits and Costs 52
Domain Names and Hosting 53
Websites and the Law 54
Success of Business Websites 55
Creating a Website 56

Section Eight — Business Applications

Word Processors: Text Formatting 57
Word Processors: Text and Graphics 58
Word Processors: Business Letters 60
Word Processors: Mail Merge 61
Spreadsheets 62
Spreadsheets: Using Formulas 63
Spreadsheets: Using Functions 64
Spreadsheets: Graphs and Charts 65
Databases 67
Databases: Data Input Forms 68
Databases: Simple Queries and Sorting 69
Databases: Producing Reports 71
Graphics: Creating Images 72
Graphics: Manipulating Images 73
Presentation Software 74
Presentations 75
Web-Authoring Software 76
Other Software Applications 77
Evaluating Software 78

Assessment Skills

Controlled Assessment 79
Exam Marks 81
Sample Exam Questions 83

If you see this symbol next to a question, it means you need to use a **computer** to answer it. For some of these questions, you'll also need some extra **data files**. There's more about these questions (and details of where to find the data files) on the **inside front cover** of this book. Yeah, that one about two pages back.

Published by Coordination Group Publications Ltd.

Editors:
Helena Hayes
Andy Park
Dave Ryan
Michael Southorn

Contributors:
Peter Cunningham

Colin Harber Stuart

With thanks to *Simon Little* and *Victoria Skelton* for the proofreading.

ISBN: 978 1 84762 321 8

Groovy website: www.cgpbooks.co.uk

Printed by Elanders Hindson Ltd, Newcastle upon Tyne.
Jolly bits of clipart from CorelDRAW®

Microsoft product screen shots reprinted with permission from Microsoft Corporation.

Based on the classic CGP style created by Richard Parsons.

Text, design, layout and original illustrations © Coordination Group Publications Ltd. 2009
All rights reserved.

SECTION ONE — BUSINESS ESSENTIALS

Why Businesses Exist

Q1 Read the text below and then answer the following question.

> Karen Booth is opening a small sandwich shop in Nantwich, Cheshire. In her first year, Karen aims to break even. For the years after that, Karen has decided on a number of objectives, some financial, and others non-financial.

Suggest two possible **financial** objectives and two possible **non-financial** objectives for Karen.

Financial objectives	Non-financial objectives
1.	1. ....
2.	2. ....

Q2 Complete the sentences below, using words or phrases from the box to fill in the spaces.

> cover their costs   non-financial   not-for-profit   financial   increase profits
> paid out to shareholders   private sector   put back into the business   help other people

a) Most businesses will only pursue .... objectives if they will also .... in the long run.

b) .... organisations aim to make enough money to .... Any surplus is ....

Q3 How are social enterprises different from most businesses?

....

....

Q4 Which **two** of the following would be the **most likely** reasons why someone would want to start their own business?

a) So they can pay less income tax. ☐
b) The independence of being their own boss. ☐
c) To reduce the number of hours they have to work. ☐
d) They have a great idea for a new product or service. ☐
e) To prove to their friends that they've got the drive to succeed. ☐

The existence of businesses — I have video evidence...

Or at least I did, until my mum recorded over it with one of her Sunday night gentle-comedy-dramas. Nothing too tricky on this first page — and now you're nicely warmed up, I reckon you should have a crack at page 2.

Enterprise

Q1 Tick whether each of the following statements about enterprise activity is **true** or **false**.

		True	False
a)	Enterprise involves identifying new business opportunities.	☐	☐
b)	Entrepreneurs often look for a gap in the market for a new product or service.	☐	☐
c)	Entrepreneurs avoid market niches as large companies usually dominate them.	☐	☐
d)	Entrepreneurs might help existing companies expand by coming up with new ideas.	☐	☐
e)	The reward for successful enterprise activity is profit.	☐	☐

Q2 Explain what is meant by taking a **calculated risk**.

....
....
....

Q3 Which **two** of the following qualities do you think are most important for an entrepreneur to have?

a) A willingness to study for a business qualification. ☐
b) The ability to learn from past mistakes. ☐
c) Willingness to be the owner of a large business. ☐
d) The ability to do complex financial calculations. ☐
e) Having the initiative to seize business opportunities. ☐

There must have been something wrong with my calculations. This wasn't supposed to happen.

Q4 Use the information in the box below to answer the following questions.

> In 2007, journalist Jake Harte set up his ethical shoe company, Harte & Sole after realising that there was a gap in the market for fashionable vegan-friendly and ethically produced shoes. After visiting many trade shows, he managed to convince several manufacturers to provide him with just the shoes he needs, in small quantities so he never needs to hold much stock at home, where he runs the business from a small office. Using his contacts as a journalist, Jake was able to get the endorsement of several popular celebrities and has since seen his profits grow month after month.

a) Explain what made Jake's idea a **good business idea**.

....
....

b) Identify two enterprise skills shown by Jake.

1. ....

2. ....

Section One — Business Essentials

Business Ownership Structures

Q1 Which of the following statements are **true**?

a) A sole trader usually has a partner to take care of running the business. ☐
b) Being a sole trader means you get to decide what to do with the profits of the business. ☐
c) A sole trader can't lose more money than they've invested in the business. ☐
d) It's easy for a partnership to expand by making shares available for anyone to buy. ☐
e) In a partnership, each owner is legally responsible for what all the other partners do. ☐
f) Partnerships are usually unincorporated and have unlimited liability. ☐

Q2 Lisa and Paul have both written a definition of limited liability. Tick the correct definition.

The maximum amount that the owners of a business can lose if the business fails is equal to the amount they have invested in the business.

Lisa ☐

Limited liability means that the maximum amount the owners of a business can lose if the business fails is equal to the current value of their shareholding.

Paul ☐

Q3 Read the text below and then answer the question that follows.

Sid and Fred own Deeply Dishy Ltd. — a firm which installs TV aerials. The demand for installation has fallen over the last six months. They have outstanding debts with their aerial supplier and are unsure whether they'll be able to pay their staff at the end of each month.

Are Sid and Fred personally liable for the firm's debts? Explain your answer.

Think about the ownership structure of Deeply Dishy.

....
....
....
....

Q4 Join each ownership structure on the left to the correct statement on the right.

Private Limited Company   Shares can only be sold if all the shareholders agree

Public Limited Company   Shares can be bought and sold by anybody

Q5 Frank is opening a franchise of Kolestro-Burger, a fast food company.

Explain what is meant by a 'franchise'.

....
....

Section One — Business Essentials

Customers

Q1 Businesses may be **market-driven** or **product-driven**.

a) Explain what a market-driven business would do before making a product.

....

....

b) Explain why a market-driven approach is often better than a product-driven approach.

....

....

Q2 Which of the following statements about customer service is true? Tick the correct box.

a) Good customer service can lead to customers making repeat purchases of a product. ☐

b) Customer service is unimportant after a firm's product has been purchased. ☐

c) A business has little to gain from providing good customer service. ☐

d) Only firms that sell expensive products can afford to provide good customer service. ☐

Q3 A firm sells electrical kitchen appliances through its website. Which of the statements below are examples of good customer service? Explain your answers.

a) 75% of the firm's products are dispatched within four days of the given dispatch date.

Good customer service?   Yes ☐   No ☐

Explanation: ....

....

b) The firm's call centre currently responds to 80% of customer telephone enquiries.

Good customer service?   Yes ☐   No ☐

Explanation: ....

....

Q4 Explain how an increase in a firm's spending on customer service can lead to an increase in profits.

....

....

....

....

Section One — Business Essentials

Stakeholders

Q1 Define the term 'stakeholder'.

....

Q2 Divide the stakeholders in the box below into **internal** and **external** stakeholders. Write them in the correct column in the table.

> owners   customers   suppliers   directors
> employees   local community   government

Internal Stakeholders	External Stakeholders

Q3 Explain how a firm's competitors can be considered stakeholders in the firm.

....

Q4 Steve has recently bought a pub in a quiet residential area of town.
State how each of the following could affect both the **business** and its **wider stakeholders**.

a) The pub plays loud music until the early hours of the morning most nights.

....
....
....

b) The drinks are cheaper than other pubs in the area.

....
....
....

c) The workers are paid well and have lots of benefits.

....
....
....

Section One — Business Essentials

Measuring Business Success

Q1 Match each term on the left to its correct definition on the right.

Success criteria — The targets a business uses to measure whether or not it has met its objectives.

Strategy — The way that a business co-ordinates the activities of each department in order to try to achieve its objectives.

Q2 Which of the following best supports the claim that a business has met its objective of behaving in an ethical way?

a) The firm now markets itself as a morally responsible business. ☐

b) The business now gets all its raw materials from fair trade sources. ☐

c) 85% of the firm's customers are happy with the standard of customer service they receive. ☐

d) The business has made record profits, and some of the shareholders would like to donate a portion of the profits to charity. ☐

Yeah, we're mostly involved in murders and executions.
What?!
Mergers and acquisitions.

Q3 Firms often use changes in their **market share** to measure success.

a) Explain what is meant by market share.

....

....

b) Give **two** ways a firm can be affected by one of its competitors increasing its market share.

1. ....

2. ....

Q4 Read the text below and then answer the question that follows.

> Durden's Soap Plc. is a soap manufacturer with a factory in the south-east of England. In the 12 months up to 31st March 2009, the firm took on 20 new members of staff and increased its output of soap by 15%. They also raised prices slightly across their whole range of products. As a result, the company's takings increased by 10% over the previous year. Despite this increase in revenue, Durden's profits were slightly down on the previous year, mainly due to their increased wage bill and the firm's new environmental policy. This policy involves cleaning up pollution in the area around their factory, and trying to use raw materials from more sustainable sources.

Discuss why the stakeholders of Durden's Soaps may have different views about how successful the firm was in this year.

government   shareholders
consumers   local community

Think about how these different groups of stakeholders might feel about the firm's activity throughout the year.

Section One — Business Essentials

Starting a New Business

Q1 Which of the following statements are true?

a) Innovation is another word for invention. ☐

b) In business, an invention can either be an idea for a new product or for a new way of doing something. ☐

c) For a new business to succeed, it must usually offer something that is not being provided by other businesses. ☐

d) All new ideas are innovative. ☐

Lucy and Johnny were impressed by Mrs Frostick's innovative teaching style.

"Good morning, children!"

Q2 What is meant by a USP (unique selling point)?

....
....

Q3 There are many ways a firm can **add value** to a product.

a) Explain what '**adding value**' to a product means.

....
....

b) How can good **design** and **quality** add value to a product?

....
....

c) Explain why having a strong **brand image** means a firm can charge more for a product.

....
....

Q4 Explain how a manufacturer's 'quick cook' pasta might have added value over its regular pasta.

....
....
....

Bargain snakeskin boots — no, that's adder value...

Gee, there's a lot for an entrepreneur to think about. I don't have the drive for it myself, that's why I ~~ended up doing this~~ chose to write questions about business studies instead...only kidding — I live for this stuff.

Section One — Business Essentials

Succeeding as a New Start-Up

Q1 Explain why some manufacturing firms may choose to locate closer to their customers than to their suppliers.

....
....
....

Q2 What are the advantages to a business of locating near to an area of high unemployment?

....
....
....

Q3 Which **two** of the following do you think would be **most important** when a firm is choosing a location?

- a) Being in an area that has a fast and reliable internet service. ☐
- b) Being close to good transport links. ☐
- c) Being in an area of natural beauty. ☐
- d) Being close to leisure facilities for workers like shops, restaurants and gyms. ☐

Q4 Colin Grover has come up with a design for a self-cleaning frying pan. Colin is afraid that his idea will be copied by a large firm before he has a chance to start production of his pan.

a) Explain how Colin could protect his design from being copied.

....
....

b) Colin has produced some leaflets advertising his product. What stops another company from copying the wording of Colin's leaflets?

....
....

Q5 Does a good business plan guarantee that a business will be successful? Explain your answer.

> Sorry — I seem to have run out of page here. You'll have to grab yourself some paper to scribble the mini-essay answer to this question.

Parrots make great entrepreneurs — they love to succeed...

Succeed... suck seed... get it? Oh never mind. It can be hard for a business trying to make it in the big wide world. Make sure you know what the business can do to give itself the best possible chance of succeeding.

Section One — Business Essentials

Businesses and the Law

Q1 Which of the following are **not** a part of employment law?

a) Employees must be given at least one day off at the weekend. ☐

b) Staff must be paid at least the national minimum wage. ☐

c) Employers can't discriminate unfairly against candidates when recruiting. ☐

d) Staff are not permitted to work more than 40 hours in a week. ☐

Q2 Explain how a business might benefit from Health and Safety legislation.

....

....

Q3 Explain why each of the following would be illegal under Sale of Goods Legislation.

a) Selling a pen that writes well, but leaks ink.

....

....

b) Selling a washing-up liquid that does not get dishes clean.

....

....

c) Selling ten bread rolls in a packet that is labelled as containing twelve rolls.

....

....

Q4 There are many laws which regulate how businesses use information and electronic data. Do you think each of the following is **always** illegal? Explain your answers.

a) A business buys a word-processing software package and installs a copy on each of its employee's machines.

b) A firm sends marketing text messages to customers.

c) A business uses an image from the internet in its advertising.

d) A business uses the internet to find out from the local council why their planning permission application has been refused.

Quite a long 'un this — you'll have to write your answer on a separate bit of paper I'm afraid.

I've found a great picture online for our new ad campaign, boss.

Hmm... I love lolcats as much as the next man, Ryan — but are they going to help us sell life insurance?

It's not a sick parrot — it's an ill eagle...

Two jokes about parrots on consecutive pages — I'm on a roll today. Back to business though, and you need to know how all these laws affect businesses, and what they've got to do to stick to them.

Section One — Business Essentials

SECTION TWO — MARKETING AND FINANCE

Marketing and Market Research

Q1 There are four Ps which together make up the **marketing mix** — product, price, promotion and place. Which **two** of the following statements are most important to the marketing mix?

- a) The product should fulfil customers' needs or wants. ☐
- b) The product should include new technology. ☐
- c) The product should be priced more cheaply than all competing products. ☐
- d) Promotion should make potential customers aware that the product exists. ☐
- e) The promotion for a product should be seen by everybody in the population. ☐
- f) The product should be available to buy in High Street shops. ☐

Q2 Explain why a business may need to adapt its marketing mix over time.

....

....

....

Q3 Which of the following are **disadvantages** of using secondary research? Tick the correct boxes.

- a) It needs a large sample group to give meaningful results. ☐
- b) It is not always relevant to the needs of the business. ☐
- c) It's very time consuming to collect data. ☐
- d) The data may be out of date. ☐
- e) The research may not be about the firm's products. ☐
- f) It can be very expensive because lots of people are needed to collect the data. ☐

Q4 Complete each of the following statements using a word from the box below.

| secondary | qualitative | field | quantitative | primary |

- a) Information that can be reduced to a number is called .... data.
- b) Information about people's views and opinions is called .... data.
- c) Looking for data in newspapers is a type of .... research.

Q5 Explain why qualitative data can be difficult to analyse.

....

....

Analysing the Market

Q1 The word 'market' can mean the group of potential customers for a product.

a) Explain what is meant by a 'market segment'.

....

b) Give **two** examples of market segments.

1. ....

2. ....

Q2 New businesses often map the market to try to find a **gap in the market**.

a) Explain what is meant by a 'gap in the market'.

....

....

b) Explain how analysing the strengths and weaknesses of competitors can help a new business become competitive.

....

....

Q3 A new business needs to research existing products before it enters a market.

a) Suggest how researching the **price** of existing products might help a business successfully launch a similar product.

....

....

b) How might researching competitors' prices help a firm spot a gap in the market?

....

....

Q4 Crazy Juice Ltd is analysing its sales data for 2008. It has produced a bar chart showing revenue from sales of apple juice throughout the year.

Bar chart showing monthly sales of apple juice in 2008

Describe how the revenue figures change throughout the year.
Suggest how they could increase their revenue in winter.

Section Two — Marketing and Finance

Prices, Revenue, Costs and Profit

Q1 Here is a list of statements about the laws of demand and supply.
Tick the pair of statements which are **both** correct.

LAW OF DEMAND	LAW OF SUPPLY	
A: Demand increases when price increases	Supply increases when demand increases	☐
B: Demand decreases when price increases	Price increases when supply increases	☐
C: Demand increases when price decreases	Supply increases when price increases	☐
D: Demand increases when supply decreases	Supply increases when demand decreases	☐

Q2 Draw lines to join each term to the description on the right that matches it best.

- Indirect costs — Expenses attributed to making a particular product.
- Variable costs — Expenses that increase as output increases.
- Fixed costs — The general overheads of running a business.
- Direct costs — Expenses that stay the same when output changes.

Q3 Tick the correct box to say what type of cost each of the following are. Explain your answers.

a) The cost of raw materials.　　Direct cost ☐　　Indirect cost ☐

　　Explanation: ....

b) The cost of office rent.　　Fixed cost ☐　　Variable cost ☐

　　Explanation: ....

Q4 BaggitUp makes 20,000 gift bags at a total cost of £17,500. All 20,000 are sold at a price of £1.50 each. Tick whether the following statements are true or false.

　　　　　　　　　　　　　　　　　　　　　　　　　　　　　　　　　　　　True　False

a) BaggitUp's total revenue is £20,000.　　☐　☐

b) After subtracting total costs from revenue, the firm is left with £12,500 profit.　　☐　☐

c) If the selling price of each bag had been any lower, they would not have made a profit.　　☐　☐

d) BaggitUp made a profit of £2,500.　　☐　☐

e) If only 12,000 bags had been sold, the firm would not have made a profit.　　☐　☐

Q5 BaggitUp have made a **spreadsheet** to compare their costs, sales and revenues with those of competing companies that sell similar bags.

To complete this question, you'll need the spreadsheet file **BaggitUp**. Check out the inside front cover to find out where to get it from.

This is the kind of question you might find in your computer-based assessment, so I'd have a crack at doing it if I were you.

a) Add **equations** to columns D, G and H to show the 'indirect costs', 'revenue' and 'profit' columns.

b) Which company made the most profit? Which companies (if any) made a loss?

c) Add **equations** to row 10 to show the 'average' of each of the quantities.

Section Two — Marketing and Finance

Finance and Cash Flow

Q1 Describe **one** source of long-term finance and **one** source of short-term finance that might be available to people starting up a new business.

Long-term: ....

....

Short-term: ....

....

Q2 What is the difference between **internal** and **external** sources of finance? Give an example of each.

....

....

Q3 Explain why using a cash flow forecast might be useful for a business.

....

....

Q4 Complete the cash flow table for Yoo Too Sunglasses Ltd. below.

Cash Flow Statement — Yoo Too Sunglasses Ltd.							
£	February	March	April	May	June	July	August
Total receipts (cash inflow)	300	350	1000	1300		1500	1300
Total payments (cash outflow)	1000	1200	1300		1250	300	200
Net cash flow	**-700**		**-300**	**-50**	150	1200	1100
Cumulative cash flow	600	**-250**		**-600**	**-450**	750	

Q5 Suggest **two** ways in which a business could improve its cash flow.

1. ....

2. ....

Want to improve your cash flow? Invest in a slide...

I know what you're thinking — we've all got cash flow problems. Unfortunately, businesses can't always rely on the bank of Mum and Dad to lend them a tenner when they're a bit skint. Pity, really.

Section Two — Marketing and Finance

The Economic Environment

Q1 Economic growth often follows a pattern called the **business cycle**.

a) Draw the regular pattern of the business cycle on the diagram below. Label your business cycle to show booms and recessions.

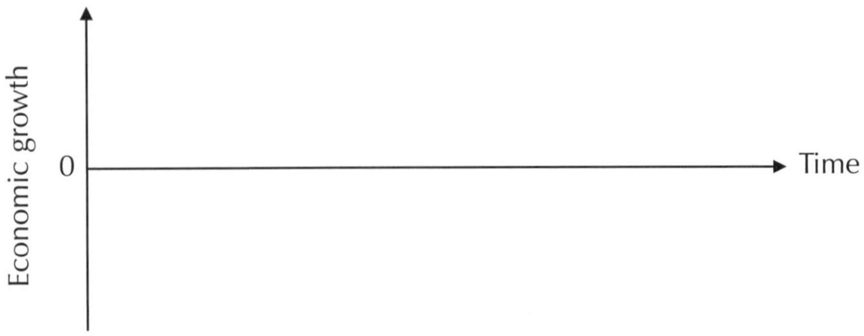

(Diagram: axes labelled "Economic growth" (vertical) and "Time" (horizontal), origin 0)

Speech bubble: The business cycle is perfect for laundering your filthy cash — even at low temperatures.

b) Explain why a small business might have more problems during a recession than a large business.

....

....

Q2 Are the following statements about interest rates true or false? Tick the correct boxes.

		True	False
a)	A high interest rate means you will pay back less money on a loan than you would at a low interest rate.	☐	☐
b)	A high interest rate means you will earn more money on a savings account than you would at a low interest rate.	☐	☐

Q3 In this question, the exchange rate between pounds and dollars is **£1 = $1.70**. Use this information to fill in the missing values in the table below.

You can use a calculator for this question.

	Product	Price in pounds (£)	Price in dollars ($)
a)	Scissors	£5.00	$ ....
b)	Magazine	£	$5.95
c)	DVD recorder	£125.00	$ ....

Q4 Pimlico Pools Plc. is a British company which makes children's paddling pools. The firm imports many of its raw materials from overseas. It sells its products both in foreign countries and in the UK. Explain how changing exchange rates could affect Pimlico Pools.

....

....

I simply don't believe that you could fully answer this question on just two lines. You'd best grab an alternative writing surface to finish your answer off.

Section Two — Marketing and Finance

SECTION THREE — ORGANISATION & ADMINISTRATION

Organisational Structure

Q1 Draw lines from each job role on the left to its description on the right.

- Supervisor — Not responsible for any other workers. Given specific tasks to complete.
- Manager — Looking after specific projects or small teams of workers.
- Operative — Responsible for organising the activities involved in carrying out the firm's strategy.
- Director — Decides the firm's strategy and targets.

Q2 This question is about the structure of organisations.

Label each of the organisation charts below, using one of the labels from the following box.

| tall hierarchy | circular chart | flat hierarchy | matrix structure |

For each of the organisation structures, suggest how the structure might affect business **communication**.

a) Name: ....

Effect on communication: ....

b) Name: ....

Effect on communication: ....

c) Name: ....

Effect on communication: ....

d) Name: ....

Effect on communication: ....

Q3 Using a suitable piece of software, produce a chart to show the structure of an organisation you know well.

Check out the inside front cover of this book to find out what the heck is going on with this question.

- Schools are examples of hierarchies. You could draw a chart to show the structure of the **whole** school, or maybe just a **part** of it (e.g. the Business Studies or ICT department).
- You'll need to use software that will let you draw lines and shapes, and also use text.

Administration in Business

Q1 Below are four steps involved in administration. Write down which of these steps each of the activities described is an example of.

Storing   **Processing**   **Retrieving**   **Disseminating**

a) Staff being sent an e-mail about changes to their firm's fire safety policy. ....

b) An accountant putting a firm's financial records into a filing cabinet. ....

c) A manager giving a slideshow presentation on last year's sales figures. ....

d) A chef finding records of last month's orders... ....

e) ...to work out what stock he needs this month. ....

Q2 When an operative at a call centre answers a call from a customer, they usually ask for their name or account number. This is then used to retrieve information about that customer from a database.

a) Describe how efficient retrieval of customers' details allows the firm to deliver better customer service.

....

....

b) Give **two** other examples of how good administration can help a company become more competitive.

1. ....

....

2. ....

....

Q3 Explain what each tax below is and what information a firm needs to keep in its records to make sure it pays the correct amount.

a) Income Tax: ....

....

....

b) Value Added Tax (VAT): ....

....

....

c) Corporation Tax: ....

....

Section Three — Organisation & Administration

Routine & Non-Routine Tasks

Q1 Tick whether each of the following statements is **true** or **false**.

	True	False
a) Non-routine tasks may involve high-level decision making.	☐	☐
b) Re-designing an existing product would be a routine task.	☐	☐
c) An increasing use of ICT means that most non-routine tasks are now carried out by computers.	☐	☐

Q2 Tick the boxes next to the tasks below which are **routine tasks**.

- choosing where to build a new factory ☐
- changing the till roll at a cashier's desk ☐
- designing an advert for a new product ☐
- replacing an ink cartridge in a printer ☐
- interviewing candidates for a job ☐
- inputting phone numbers onto a database ☐

Q3 Explain why developing a new product is an example of a non-routine task.

....
....
....

Q4 For each of the decisions below, decide who from the following list is **most likely** to make the decision.

| restaurant manager | chef | a computer |

Today's special will be... MICROCHIPS! HAHAHA. Why are you not ROFLing? Does not compute.

a) Choosing a new head chef.

Decision likely to be made by: ....

Explanation: ....
....

b) Choosing dishes for the 'specials' menu.

Decision likely to be made by: ....

Explanation: ....
....

Section Three — Organisation & Administration

Planning

Q1 Match each word on the left to the correct definition on the right.

Planning — Deciding which tasks are most important and dealing with them sooner.

Prioritising — Thinking about what needs to be achieved and working out the best way to do it with the resources available.

Q2 Decide if each of the following statements about planning is true or false.

		True	False
a)	Good planning can increase a firm's efficiency.	☐	☐
b)	Firms never use information from past projects when planning projects for the future	☐	☐
c)	Good planning means a firm will be prepared for all possible problems.	☐	☐
d)	The best laid plans of mice and men often go astray.	☐	☐

Q3 Describe how bad planning may affect each of the following aspects of a project:

a) Timing ....
....

b) Cost ....
....

c) Quality ....
....

Q4 Explain how each of the following can help when planning a project:

a) Breaking the project down into a series of smaller tasks

....
....

b) Milestones

....
....

c) Access to accurate information on similar past projects.

....
....

Witty remark here? I hadn't planned on doing one...
Turn up at the Winter Olympics without having planned a figure-skating routine and you'd look a fool (unless you're on the bobsleigh team). Similarly, firms that don't plan properly often end up with egg on their faces.

Section Three — Organisation & Administration

Efficient Use of Resources

Q1 Which of the following would best describe an efficient company? Tick your answer.

a) They make the required amount of products, with as little waste of resources as possible. ☐

b) They use a reduced workforce to produce the required amount of products. ☐

c) They recycle any waste that is made during the production process. ☐

Q2 Paula and Ryan run a recruitment agency from home. They want to expand their business by renting out an office and employing three more members of staff. Discuss which of the following offices would be most suitable for their business.

A — For rent — 8th floor of a new development, composing of 5 offices and a conference room.

B — For rent — a modern open plan office suitable for up to 30 employees, with three conference rooms.

....

....

....

....

Q3 An accounting business has a vacancy for a worker whose tasks will mainly be answering phones, filing and setting up meetings. Tick the statement below which you most agree with.

a) Employing a qualified accountant would be most efficient, because they know how the business works and will be able to work much faster. ☐

b) It would be more efficient to get somebody who is cheaper to employ to do the job, because the tasks are fairly simple and don't require a qualified accountant to complete them. ☐

Q4 Explain how using resources and energy more efficiently can have an effect on the environment.

....

....

Q5 Jolly Hols Travel are a travel agent with 6 shops in the UK. They are currently looking to replace their computer system. Below is the opinion of one of their members of staff.

"I think the company should get computers that are really cheap. I'm worried that if they spend too much money on the computers they might get into financial trouble and I might lose my job."

The directors of Jolly Hols Travel have asked you to write a memo to explain to employees the benefits to the company of buying more expensive computer equipment.

You should use word processing software to produce your memo. Some of these terms might help you:

short term   slow   upgrade   quality   efficiency

This is another one of those brilliant questions to help you practise for your computer-based assessment. See the inside front cover for more info.

Section Three — Organisation & Administration

Office Layout

Q1 The two main types of office layout are listed below. Describe the main features of each, and explain **one** advantage and **one** disadvantage.

Layout	Main features	Advantage	Disadvantage
Open plan offices			
Cellular offices			

Q2 Recommend what type of office layout the following businesses might choose. Justify your answers.

a) A marketing company where employees work in large teams.

....

....

b) A company that provides a walk-in advice service for individuals with debt problems.

....

....

Q3 Tina is the office manager for an accountancy firm. She has recently ordered a range of ergonomically designed office equipment for the firm's workers.

a) Explain what is meant by 'ergonomically designed'.

....

....

b) Explain the possible benefits to the business of introducing this new equipment.

....

....

....

I always type lying down — I'm an office layabout...

That was nice and easy — just two types of layout. In the exam you'll be expected to know the advantages and disadvantages of both as well. Oh, and have a couple of examples of firms that might use each type too.

Section Three — Organisation & Administration

SECTION FOUR — HUMAN RESOURCES

Patterns of Work

Q1 Tick whether each of the following statements about part-time employment is **true** or **false**.

		True	False
a)	An increasing number of businesses now offer employees flexible working hours.	☐	☐
b)	Part-time and full-time workers have equal employment rights.	☐	☐
c)	Some people prefer to work part-time to spend more time with their family.	☐	☐
d)	More people are now choosing to work part time.	☐	☐
e)	Part-time workers usually work around 40 hours a week.	☐	☐

Q2 Use the words in the box below to complete the following sentences. You do not need to use all the words.

> qualifications   a fixed period   harder   rights
> job security   student workers   easier   end date

a) A permanent contract of employment has no ....

b) Temporary workers will find it .... to get a mortgage than permanent workers.

c) A temporary contract is for ....

Q3 Explain why employing temporary workers can have benefits for a business.

....
....
....

Q4 List **six** pieces of information you would expect to find on a **written contract of employment**.

1. ....   2. ....
3. ....   4. ....
5. ....   6. ....

Q5 Abby is a qualified teacher looking for work. She is unsure whether to accept a permanent teaching position or whether to join an agency which would find her regular temporary work. Discuss the advantages and disadvantages to Abby of both permanent and temporary contracts.

> redundancy   renew   wages   risk

These terms to the left might be useful to put into your answer. It'll impress the examiners. Which is no bad thing marks-wise.

Oh dear, no room at the inn. You'll have to find somewhere else to put your answer. Try writing on a banana skin with a felt tip. Curiously satisfying.

Section Four — Human Resources

Recruitment — Job Analysis

Q1 What is the difference between a **job description** and a **person specification**?

....
....
....

Q2 Write each of the headings below on the correct document.

- Experience
- Responsible for
- Main purpose of job
- Skills
- Desirable qualities
- Job title
- Qualifications
- Attitudes
- Reports to
- Essential qualities
- Duties

Job Description
- ....
- ....
- ....
- ....
- ....
- ....

Person Specification
- ....
- ....
- ....
- ....
- ....
- ....

Q3 Sally is the manager of a department store. One of her junior managers is leaving. Sally is planning on advertising for a replacement internally by posting a job advert on the staff notice board.

a) Suggest **five** pieces of information **about the job** that might be included in the advert.
You should **not** use any of the headings from Q2.

1. ....
2. ....
3. ....
4. ....
5. ....

b) Explain **one** advantage and **one** disadvantage of Sally only advertising the post internally, rather than externally as well.

Advantage: ....
....

Disadvantage: ....
....

Section Four — Human Resources

Recruitment — The Selection Process

Q1 A curriculum vitae (or CV) is sometimes used in the selection process for a job. Write down **three** things that might appear on a candidate's CV.

1. .... 2. .... 3. ....

Q2 Businesses sometimes ask candidates to fill in an **application form**.

a) Why might large businesses prefer to receive an application form rather than a letter of application?

....
....
....

b) What kind of things do you think a firm looks for in a good application?

....
....

Q3 Below are some things that an employer might look for in a potential employee. Tick whether each is a **skill** or an **attitude**.

	Skill	Attitude
a) An enthusiastic approach to work.	☐	☐
b) Able to work in both small and large teams.	☐	☐
c) Able to use spreadsheet software.	☐	☐
d) Happy to help out when co-workers are busy.	☐	☐
e) Able to write in shorthand.	☐	☐

Q4 Firms often use written applications to make a short-list of potential job candidates — these candidates will then be invited for an interview. Explain **one** disadvantage of interviewing candidates.

....
....

Q5 You have been asked by BluSkyThought Ltd to write a set of letters inviting short-listed job applicants to an interview. The letters will be produced using **mail merge**.

Your letter should:
- follow the **standard format** for a business letter
- include **merge fields** linked to the spreadsheet of applicants' details.
- include BluSkyThought's address and the sender's name and position

Remember to check through your mail-merged letters for mistakes.

You'll need the files 'BluSkyLetter' and 'BluSkySpreadsheet' to help you answer this question. See the inside front cover of this book to find out where to get 'em.

Section Four — Human Resources

Employment Law

Q1 Employees must be given a written contract of employment within two months of them starting a new job. What other document must also be made available to them within the first two months?

....

Q2 List **six** things about a candidate or employee that, by law, employers are not allowed to use as a basis for **discrimination**.

1. .... 2. .... 3. ....

4. .... 5. .... 6. ....

Q3 Ben is the manager of a restaurant. Steve works for Ben as a waiter. One evening, Steve accidentally drops a plate of food on the floor.

a) Is it legal for Ben to dismiss Steve for this? Yes ☐ No ☐

b) Explain your answer.

....

....

Q4 What is the only reason that an employee can be made **redundant** from their job?

....

Q5 If a person feels they have been **unfairly** dismissed what legal action can they take? What might they be able to achieve by doing this?

....

....

Q6 Explain how employment laws can have drawbacks for a **business**.

....

....

....

Section Four — Human Resources

Staff Training

Q1 Most businesses give their employees **induction training**.

a) When does induction training occur? Tick the correct box.

- Throughout a worker's employment. ☐
- At the start of a worker's employment. ☐
- Whenever a new skill needs to be learned. ☐

b) Explain the main purposes of induction training.

....

....

Q2 Many businesses give their staff **on-the-job** training. Write down one advantage and one disadvantage that this training method can have for a business.

Advantage: ....

Disadvantage: ....

Q3 SilkiSoft is a company that produces video games. It sometimes sends its programming staff to courses at a local university to learn new skills.

a) What is the name given to training that takes place outside the business?

....

b) How might SilkiSoft's staff benefit from being trained at the university rather than at work?

....

c) Give one disadvantage to SilkiSoft of training its staff away from the workplace.

....

Q4 Explain **three** benefits of staff training for both **employers** and the **employees** of a firm.

Benefits of training to employers	Benefits of training to employees
1.	1. ....
2.	2. ....
3.	3. ....

Section Four — Human Resources

Financial Rewards

Q1   Most businesses pay their employees for their work.

   a) Explain the difference between **wages** and **salaries**.

   ....
   ....

   b) Give **one** advantage and **one** disadvantage to a firm
      of giving their employees a salary rather than a wage.

      Advantage: ....

      Disadvantage: ....

Q2   The box below contains three methods used for paying workers. For each occupation in the table, decide which is the most appropriate method and explain your choice.

   time rate   piece rate   commission

	Occupation	Method of Payment	Explanation
a)	Train driver	....	....
b)	Textiles worker making hand-made cushions	....	....
c)	Double-glazing salesperson	....	....

Q3   Commission and bonuses are two types of performance-related pay. Explain the difference between commission and bonuses.

   ....
   ....

Q4   Explain what is meant by an **overtime rate**.

   ....
   ....

Section Four — Human Resources

Financial Rewards

Q1 What is the difference between **gross pay** and **net pay**?

....

....

Q2 An employee earns a gross salary of £1240 per month. He pays 5% of his gross salary into a pension fund. How much does he pay into his pension each month?

Working out what 1% of his pay is first will make your life easier.

....

....

....

Q3 A worker currently earns a time-rate wage of £9 per hour. He is being given a 3% pay rise. Calculate his new hourly wage.

....

....

....

Q4 Some firms offer their staff **fringe benefits**.

a) What is meant by a fringe benefit?

Congratulations Perkins, you've met your sales targets for three consecutive quarters — it's time to collect your fringe benefit.

....

....

b) Explain how offering its employees a staff discount can benefit **both** a firm and its employees.

....

....

Q5 Domino Confectionery are introducing a range of fringe benefits for their staff.

You have been asked to design a poster that can be put up on noticeboards around the company's offices informing employees of the scheme.
You can choose any **three** benefits to include on your poster.

Your poster should:
- explain the fringe benefits that are being offered
- be eye-catching
- include images and text
- be made using suitable software.

I'm sure you know by now that these questions are great practice for the computer-based exam. If not, check out the details on the inside front cover.

Section Four — Human Resources

Modern Working Practices

Q1   Gerald is the manager of a small graphic design firm.

a) He has recently introduced flexitime for his workers. Describe what is meant by flexitime and explain **one** way in which flexitime could have a negative effect on the business.

....

....

b) Gerald is also considering allowing his staff to telework.

i) What is meant by **teleworking**?

....

ii) Give **one** benefit and **one** drawback this might have for his **employees**.

Benefit: ....

....

Drawback: ....

....

Q2   Creativ-Ads is an advertising company whose staff work in regularly changing project teams. The firm's employees work at hot-desks. Explain what is meant by **hot-desking** and the advantages it has for Creative-Ads.

....

....

....

....

Q3   Above Board is a law firm with offices in Edinburgh, Manchester, Birmingham and London. The managers from each of the four offices take part in a weekly update meeting using teleconferencing.

a) What is meant by **teleconferencing**?

....

b) Explain why the managers of Above Board use teleconferencing rather than meeting in person.

....

....

c) Suggest **two** possible drawbacks of using teleconferencing.

1. ....

2. ....

Section Four — Human Resources

Health and Safety at Work

Q1 Name three things that **employees** should do to reduce health and safety risks at work.

If you need some hints, think about the rules set out by the Health and Safety at Work Act 1974.

1. ....
2. ....
3. ....

Q2 By law, firms must record any workplace injuries in an accident book. Explain why using accident books might help reduce the number of injuries that happen in workplaces.

....

....

....

Q3 List **three** health problems that may affect employees who use computers for long periods of time.

1. ....
2. ....
3. ....

Hint: Being sucked into an alternate digital universe isn't one of the three answers.

Q4 All employees at E-Quick use a computer as part of their job. The manager wants to give a **presentation** to tell staff about reducing the risks associated with computer use. Using suitable software, create a **slideshow** to accompany this presentation.

Your slideshow should include information on the following:
- techniques staff can use to help avoid health problems
- E-Quick's responsibilities to provide a safe environment for the employees to work in
- precautions both the firm and its employees can take to reduce health risks

Your slides don't have to be too in-depth — just summarise a few key points.

If you don't have a computer with presentation software, you can make your slides the old-fashioned way with pens and paper. Retro.

You can jot your ideas down here.

Section Four — Human Resources

Data Processing Systems

Q1 Business data can come from lots of different sources.
What is the difference between **primary data** and **secondary data**?

....

....

Q2 Data systems can be paper-based rather than computer-based.
Give **two** benefits and **two** drawbacks of using a paper-based data system.

Benefits	Drawbacks
1.	1. ....
2.	2. ....

Q3 Which of the following statements about computer-based data systems are true?

a) They require even more storage space than paper-based systems. ☐

b) They make it easier to edit documents. ☐

c) It is more difficult to create backup copies of data than with paper-based systems. ☐

d) Data can be easily shared via networks. ☐

Q4 Join each term on the left to the correct definition on the right.

[Hardware]   Programs that can be used on computers

[Software]   The physical parts of a computer system

We are the hardware crew, and we intend to mess you up. Isn't it.

Q5 Tick whether each of the following is an example of computer hardware or software.

	Hardware	Software
a) Internal hard drive	☐	☐
b) Laser printer	☐	☐
c) Spreadsheet application	☐	☐
d) Flight simulation game	☐	☐

Processing hardware gag... please wait...

Bit of a funny page this one — it's kind of an introduction to all the stuff that's coming up in the section. Don't just skim over it though, there's some important definitions 'n' stuff. Man, I love definitions 'n' stuff.

Computers and Input Devices

Q1 Which of the following are features that are often found on **Personal Digital Assistants** (PDAs)?

a) Telephone ☐
b) Touch-screen keypad ☐
c) CD-ROM drive ☐
d) Internet access ☐
e) Built-in printer ☐
f) Crushingly honest fashion advice

Q2 Liz is a newspaper journalist. She travels a lot around the country writing stories and is often away from the office. Suggest why Liz may prefer to use a laptop computer rather than a desktop.

....
....

Q3 Explain what a computer **network** is.

....
....

Q4 Keyboards are the most common example of an **input device**.

a) What is meant by an input device?

....

b) Describe how QWERTY keyboards and concept keyboards are different.

....
....

c) Suggest a suitable use for concept keyboards.

....
....

d) Name one problem associated with regular use of a computer keyboard.

....

Q5 Give one possible **benefit** and one possible **drawback** of using a mouse with a computer.

Benefit: ....

Drawback: ....

Section Five — Businesses and Data

More Input Devices

Q1 Sam runs his own website selling vintage clothing. Explain what he might use a **digital camera** for and how it might **benefit** his business.

....

....

Q2 Many firms use **scanners** in their offices.

a) What are scanners used for?

....

b) What is **Optical Character Recognition (OCR)** software?

....

....

Henry's poor character recognition made watching TV a stressful experience.

Q3 Many shops and supermarkets use EPOS devices.

a) What does EPOS stand for?

....

b) Explain how EPOS devices work and how they can be used by retailers.

....

....

....

Q4 Dean is unable to use a computer mouse or keyboard for medical reasons. Explain how he could use a microphone to help him to use a computer.

....

....

Q5 Data capture forms are used to collect and input data. They can be either manual or electronic.

a) Give an example of where an electronic data capture form might be used.

....

....

b) Many firms store data about their customers. Explain why allowing customers to fill in electronic data capture forms can help reduce errors in this data.

....

....

....

Section Five — Businesses and Data

Data Storage

Q1 Explain the **main difference** between internal and external storage devices.

....

....

Q2 Most computers have an internal hard disk.

a) Complete the following sentence using a word from the box below.

| megahertz | gigabytes | decibytes | kilohertz |

The storage capacity of a computer's internal hard disk is normally measured in ....

b) Suggest why a large company might prefer to store their information on a central server rather than on individual computers.

....

....

c) Explain why it's important to back up data from internal hard disks using an external storage device.

....

....

Q3 Portable storage devices have various uses, including backing up data. Suggest **one** other use.

....

....

Q4 What are the **advantages** of using memory cards and USB sticks as storage devices?

....

....

....

> Be amazed as I store 10,000 pages on one tiny device!

Audiences were unimpressed by Arthur's flash card tricks.

Q5 Explain **two** reasons why a firm might not allow their employees to use USB sticks.

1. ....

....

2. ....

....

Section Five — Businesses and Data

Data Storage and Back-Up

Q1 Draw lines to join each type of compact disc to its correct description on the right.

- CD-ROM — Sold as blank disks. Data can be recorded onto them once.
- CD-R — Read only disks. Often used by manufacturers to distribute their software.
- CD-RW — Sold as blank disks. Data can be written onto them and deleted many times.

Q2 Which of the following statements about DVDs are **true**?

a) Some blank DVDs can be written to and erased ☐
b) DVDs can hold much more data than CDs ☐
c) DVDs can hold about 700 GB of data ☐
d) CDs and DVDs look the same and can often be read by the same hardware ☐

Q3 Give **two** reasons why CDs and DVDs are often not ideal for storing business data.

1. ....
2. ....

Q4 Some firms use magnetic tape to back up their electronic data.
Give **one** advantage and **one** disadvantage of this method of back-up.

Advantage: ....

Disadvantage: ....

Q5 Explain what is meant by **web-based storage** and why it is an example of **remote storage**.

....
....
....

Q6 Explain why a business should keep its back-ups in a different location to their main building.

....
....

I keep losing my data — it's really getting my back-up...

That's your lot of data storage devices — know the main features of each, what they're good and bad for and when they might be used. Handy Hint #23: Old CDs make very fetching coffee table coasters. Retro chic.

Section Five — Businesses and Data

Output Devices — Printers

Q1 What is meant by an **output device**?

....

Q2 Printing out a document onto paper is usually more expensive than looking at it on screen. Suggest why firms still print out documents.

....

....

Q3 Give **two** advantages and **two** disadvantages of laser printers.

Advantages	Disadvantages
1.	1. ....
2.	2. ....

Q4 Until recently, dot-matrix printers were often used in tills at supermarket checkouts. Give **two** features of dot-matrix printers that made them suitable for this use.

1. ....

2. ....

Q5 Which of the following statements about ink-jet printers are **true**?

a) They have pretty good resolution, but generally not as good as laser printers. ☐
b) They can usually print over 10 colour pages per minute. ☐
c) They work by spraying small jets of ink through tiny nozzles onto the paper. ☐
d) They're usually a lot more expensive to buy than laser printers. ☐

Q6 Duncan Samuels needs to buy a new printer for his office. Duncan prints several large documents every day. Duncan also regularly sends out letters to his 65 customers. The printer will be shared with five other people in the office who also produce similar documents.

What type of printer would you recommend Duncan buys? Justify your answer.

No doubt your answer will need a bit more space than there is here — so find yourself a piece of paper to jot your answer on.

Section Five — Businesses and Data

More Output Devices

Q1 Monitors are one type of output device.

a) How might the type of monitor used by a graphic designer differ from that of an operative inputting numbers into a database?

....

....

b) What **advantages** do LCD monitors have over cathode-ray tube monitors?

....

....

....

Q2 On the right is a picture of an output device that can be attached to a computer.

a) Name the device.

....

b) Explain what this device does.

....

....

....

c) Give **two** drawbacks of using this output device.

1. ....

2. ....

Q3 Suggest a suitable output device for each of the following situations:

a) Audio-conferencing between people at different offices. ....

b) Viewing a document while it is being edited. ....

c) Converting a letter into a form which allows it to be posted to customers. ....

d) Presenting a power-point slideshow to a group of workers. ....

e) Listening to private medical notes on audio tape while typing them up. ....

I wish there was a device that would increase my output...

There's a veritable feast of output devices on this page for you to get your teeth stuck into. Well alright, there's only a few. But they're worth learning, so you can output loads of info about them in the exam.

Section Five — Businesses and Data

Keeping Data Secure

Q1 Give **three** reasons why data security is important to businesses.

1. ....

2. ....

3. ....

Q2 Businesses can take various measures to help them protect their data.

a) Suggest ways that a business can prevent equipment and data from being physically stolen.

....

b) Explain why many businesses give a username and password to employees who use the computer network.

....

....

c) Explain how each of the following can be used to restrict access to a computer network:

(i) Firewall

....

....

(ii) Screensaver

....

....

Q3 Matt is in charge of computer security for a large company. For each of the following problems, suggest which type of software from the box below he should install.

| Anti-adware software | Anti-virus software | Anti-spam software | Anti-spyware software |

Problem	Software
a) Programs that corrupt files and operating systems on users' computers	....
b) Software that collects personal information about the user without them knowing	....
c) Unwanted advertisements that pop-up on a user's screen	....
d) Unwanted electronic mail, often from companies advertising products	....

Section Five — Businesses and Data

Data Protection and the Law

Q1 Which of the following statements about data protection laws are true?

a) The laws only control the use of paper-based data. ☐
b) The Data Protection Act controls how data is collected, kept and used. ☐
c) Data about individuals can only be transferred to countries outside Europe. ☐
d) Individuals are allowed to restrict how certain data about them is used. ☐
e) All data about a person is kept for the duration of their life. ☐

Q2 Murray's Motors Ltd. collects information from every customer that it sells a car to. Like all businesses, it is required to comply with the Data Protection Act.

a) A customer requests to see the information that Murray's Motors hold about her. Under what conditions is she allowed to see this data?

....
....

b) Murray's Motors want to send the information they have collected about their customers to another company, who want to use the information for marketing purposes. Are there any circumstances where Murray's Motors are allowed to do this?

....
....

c) When a customer has bought a car from Murray's Motors, the firm stores data about their physical appearance (e.g. height, hair colour). Explain why this is illegal under the Data Protection Act.

....

d) Murray's Motors keep customers' data on file for 6 months and then disposes of the files by putting them in a skip. Is this legal under the Data Protection Act? If not, which principle has been broken?

....
....

Q3 The Data Protection Act gives rights to **data subjects**.

a) What is meant by a 'data subject'?

....

b) Give **two** examples of rights that data subjects have under the Data Protection Act.

1. ....
2. ....

Son, when it comes to data — always use protection...

Companies sometimes try to bamboozle you into giving them permission to use your details by saying things like: "Do not tick this box if you don't want us to not give your details to nobody". Watch out for that.

Section Five — Businesses and Data

Section Six — Communication

Purposes of Communication

Q1 Explain what is meant by **feedback** in communication and why it is important.

....

....

....

Q2 The box below contains an email message from a worker to a colleague.

a) Can you tell if Barry has read and understood Robert's email? Explain your answer.

....

....

b) Suggest how Robert might eventually be able to tell that the message has been understood?

> **From:** Robert Williamson
> **Sent:** 07 August 2009 11:17
> **To:** Barry Barlow
> **Subject:** Meeting
>
> Can we move our meeting today to 3pm?

....

....

Q3 Complete the table below by writing down one **benefit** of each communication method.

Communication medium	Benefit
Written	....
Oral	....
Visual	....

Q4 Cliff is the manager of a theatre. An event next week has been cancelled and he must inform people who have bought tickets for the event. Suggest the best way for Cliff to communicate this information to ticketholders. Explain your answer.

No room here, folks. You'll have to pop your answer elsewhere.

You need to think about the most appropriate method and medium as well as the best communication channels.

Internal and External Communication

Q1 In business, what is the difference between **internal** and **external** communication?

....
....

Q2 Decide whether each of the following is an example of **internal** or **external** communication.

		Internal	External
a)	A firm writes to the local council to request planning permission for development.	☐	☐
b)	The cleaning department of a firm puts a notice up in the company kitchen.	☐	☐
c)	A bank sends SMS messages to its customers telling them the balance of their account.	☐	☐

Q3 Explain how a **business** can benefit from good internal communication.

....
....

Q4 Give **two** examples of how a business communicates with its customers and describe the **purpose** of each communication.

1. ....
   ....

2. ....
   ....

Q5 Good external communication is important for a business. Explain how each of the following can benefit a firm.

a) Having good communication with suppliers.

....
....

b) Informing a customer in plenty of time that a product they have ordered will be delivered late.

....
....

A rumbly tummy — a form of internal communication...

The definitions for internal and external communications are nice and easy. The meaty stuff's all about why communication is important and how it can benefit a firm — think how all a firm's stakeholders are affected.

Section Six — Communication

Barriers to Communication

Q1 Below is a cutout from a letter sent by Leccy, an electricity company. The letter was sent to all households using rival electricity companies to try to encourage them to switch to Leccy.

a) Suggest two problems with the letter's content and presentation

1. ....
2. ....

in the allocated time. The changes apply to all customers who are part of the Energy Plus Saver scheme (except those customers who joined prior to 1st January 2006 and had previously been part of the Energy Saver 2000 scheme) and who pay their bills by direct debit (customers who pay their bills online will receive a 5% discount in the first 3 months and

b) Explain how these problems might reduce the letter's effectiveness.

....
....
....

Q2 Explain how emotional interference can affect communication between work colleagues.

....
....

Q3 Anna is a sales rep for a skincare manufacturer. She travels by train, visiting clients all over the UK. Anna uses her time on the train to make mobile phone calls to clients and co-workers.

a) Suggest two problems **Anna** may encounter when making these calls.

1. ....
2. ....

b) Think about the **clients** that Anna will ring when she is on the train. Explain how the above problems might affect their opinions of the firm.

....
....

Q4 Businesses will usually check all their documents for errors.

It helps me to concentrate if I check for errors with my eyes closed...

a) Explain why it's important for a firm to check their communications for errors before they are sent to customers.

....
....

b) Below is part of an email sent to a firm's staff. The text contains five spelling errors — circle each error.

> We've just recieved a phone call from the electricty company to say our power will definitly be switched off at 4pm tomorrow, so they can carry out some work. From past experiance, they usually turn the power off a bit earlier than they say. So it's important that everyone saves there work and logs off no later than 3.45pm.

Section Six — Communication

Written Communication — Letters

Q1 Suggest why a bank might choose to inform customers about changes to their bank account by letter rather than another medium.

....

....

Q2 A manager needs to inform a colleague that their meeting tomorrow is cancelled.

a) Explain why sending a letter by post might not be the best way for him to inform his colleague about the meeting being cancelled.

....

....

b) Suggest a more appropriate way he could let his colleague know about the cancellation and justify your choice.

....

....

Jack's pigeon mail delivery service was really taking off.

Q3 Cheryl runs 'pamper days' for girls aged 11-14. She confirms bookings for these days by sending two letters — one to the person who made the booking (who must be over 18) and one to the girl booked on the day, telling her all about it. Explain how the **style** of these two letters might differ.

....

....

....

Q4 Explain why business letters are generally presented in a standard format.

....

....

Q5 Why is posting a business letter not usually a **secure** communication channel?

....

....

Dear Mr Iceberg, Lettuce be friends, Yours Mr Slug...

It's good to know how to write a nice formal letter but it's just as useful to be able to look at a letter and say whether it's appropriate for its audience — ask yourself if the right language, tone and layout have been used.

Section Six — Communication

Internal Written Communication

NOTICES

Q1 Many firms use memos as part of their communications.

a) Describe what a **memo** is and suggest a use for them.

....

....

b) Give **one** advantage and **one** disadvantage of using memos.

Advantage: ....

Disadvantage: ....

c) Explain why many firms now send e-mails rather than use memos.

....

....

Q2 A firm's director has asked one of his employees to write a report on ways to reduce costs in the firm's warehouse. Explain why you would not expect a report like this to be sent to a firm's customers.

....

....

....

Q3 Mary is a manager at a firm which employs 90 staff. She is organising a staff party. Suggest **two** reasons why putting a notice on the staff notice board might be a good way to advertise the party.

1. ....

2. ....

Q4 Anita is the director of Beethcaites, a chain of gyms. Over 300 people are employed by Beethcaites. Anita is considering introducing a company newsletter which would be sent to every employee once a month. Discuss the benefits and drawbacks the newsletter could have for Beethcaites. Include the words below in your answer.

events   expensive   inform   motivation   productivity

Look's like we're outta space here — I know it's short notice but you'll have to find somewhere else to put your answer.

Section Six — Communication

More Written Communication

Q1   What are the **similarities** and **differences** between a brochure and a catalogue?

   ....
   ....
   ....
   ....

World Catalogue Pose Championship Final 2009

Q2   Say whether you think a **flyer** or **brochure** would be the most appropriate form of communication in each of the following situations. Explain your answers.

   a) A clothing firm wanting to give customers a preview of their new season's outfits.

   ....
   ....

   b) The same firm wanting to inform customers that they can get free delivery on all orders during February.

   ....
   ....

Q3   A firm's supplier will issue them with an invoice when goods have been delivered.

   a) What is the purpose of an invoice?

   ....

   b) Explain why it's important for suppliers to keep clear and accurate financial records.

   ....
   ....

Q4   Job advertisements will often ask candidates to send their curriculum vitae (CV) to the firm.

   a) Why do firms often want to see a candidate's CV?

   ....
   ....

   b) Explain why it's important for a candidate to check their CV thoroughly before sending it to a company.

   ....
   ....

Q5   Imagine you're applying for a job. Select an appropriate piece of software and produce a CV for yourself.

You might not have any exam grades to put on your CV yet — so you could put your predicted grades down instead.

Section Six — Communication

Electronic Communication

Q1 Fax machines are sometimes used to send documents quickly.

a) What is a fax machine?

....

....

b) Give **two** disadvantages of sending documents by fax rather than email.

1. ....

2. ....

Q2 Fill in the table below explaining **three** advantages and **three** disadvantages of using email as a form of communication.

Disadvantage: hard to eat doughnuts and type at the same time.

Aw, sticky keys.

Advantages	Disadvantages
1.	1. ....
2.	2. ....
3.	3. ....

Q3 Customers and firms can communicate with each other via a firm's website.

a) Suggest **two** ways in which a customer could give feedback to a business through its website.

1. ....

2. ....

b) Explain how a firm could restrict access to certain parts of its website.

....

....

c) Suggest why a firm may continue to send out information by post, even though the information is available on their website.

....

....

Section Six — Communication

Electronic Communication

Q1 SMS (Short Message Service) text messages can be sent to mobile phones.

a) Why might a firm remind a customer about a delivery date for a parcel with an SMS message rather than a letter?

....

....

....

b) Explain why text messages are not suitable for a lot of business communication.

....

....

....

Q2 What are electronic notice boards? Give an example of where they might be used.

....

....

....

Q3 Some supermarkets offer loyalty cards to their customers.

a) Explain what is meant by a supermarket **loyalty card** and how **customers** benefit from using them.

....

....

b) Explain how loyalty cards can be used by supermarkets for '**targeted marketing**'.

....

....

....

....

Q4 RFID (Radio Frequency IDentification) tags can be found on some products. Why might an RFID tag be attached to a product?

....

....

I'll send an SMS to the world...

Loyalty cards might not spring to mind when you're thinking of communication between a business and its customers — but those supermarkets can be clever little bunnies. At least everyone is a winner. Ish.

Section Six — Communication

Face-to-Face Meetings

Q1 Explain the **benefits** of two work colleagues holding a face-to-face meeting, rather than communicating by email.

....

....

....

Q2 Explain what is meant by **silent communication**.

....

....

Q3 Suggest how silent communication can affect how well a message is understood.

....

....

....

Q4 Many firms conduct appraisal meetings with their staff.

a) Explain what is meant by an '**appraisal meeting**'.

....

....

b) Why are they best done face-to-face?

....

Ethel and Cedric were pioneering the 'back-to-back, silent communication' meeting.

Q5 Annual General Meetings (AGMs) are usually held once a year by limited liability firms.

a) Describe the role of the **directors** at an AGM.

....

....

b) Discuss the ways in which these AGM meetings can be of benefit to a firm's **shareholders**.

....

....

c) Give **one** benefit and **one** drawback of holding an AGM as a face-to-face meeting.

Benefit: ....

Drawback: ....

Section Six — Communication

Other Oral Communication

Q1 Some firms allow customers to order their products by phone and through their website. Suggest why a customer might prefer to order a product over the **phone** rather than use the firm's website.

....

....

....

....

Q2 Many firms now use **teleconferencing** as a method of communication.

a) Describe the difference between audio-conferencing and video-conferencing.

....

....

b) Give **one** benefit and **one** drawback of using video-conferencing over audio-conferencing.

Benefit ....

Drawback ....

c) Explain why the use of teleconferencing is growing.

....

....

....

Q3 Firms are increasingly using the internet to communicate.

a) Describe what **webinars** are.

....

....

b) What is the main difference between webinars and **webcasts**?

....

....

c) Explain how and why a company might use **podcasts** as part of their marketing.

....

....

....

Section Six — Communication

Visual Communication

Q1 All businesses need a trading name.
Give **two** features of an effective trading name.

Here's my suggested trading name. Any objections?
InCapableHands

1. ....
2. ....

Q2 Most businesses have a logo.

a) Describe what is meant by a **logo**.

....
....

b) Explain why it's important for a firm to choose its logo carefully.

....
....

Q3 Suggest why it's important for a firm that their **adverts** fit in with the image they want to portray.

....
....

Q4 Explain why a company might use **celebrities** to endorse their products and services.

....
....

Q5 What are **slogans** and **straplines**? How can they be used by firms to boost sales?

....
....
....

Q6 This Way Up Movers are a home removal firm. Their logo is shown to the right.

a) Do you think their logo would be effective in helping the firm create an identity for themselves? Explain your answer.

You'll have to put your answer to part a) somewhere else folks.

b) Think about your comments for part a). Select an appropriate piece of software and create a **new logo** for the firm, including a graphic and the company's name. Add **callouts** to your logo to explain your design.

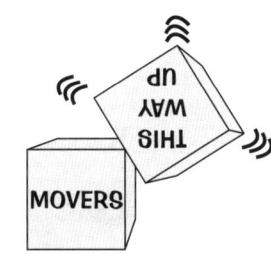

Inappropriate branding? How logo can you go...
Firms will invest lots of time thinking up a cracking name and jazzy logo so that next time you see someone eating a piece of fruit you'll have a sudden urge to go and buy an MP3 player. Ah, the wily foxes.

Section Six — Communication

Changing a Communication System

Q1 Suggest **two** reasons why a business might want to change its communication system.

1. ....

2. ....

Q2 A firm's communication systems go through a continuous cycle of change.

a) Explain why a firm might look at the faults of its existing communication systems when planning changes.

....

....

b) A firm might use an action plan when planning improvements to its communication systems. Suggest what sort of information might be included in this action plan.

....

....

c) Explain why it's important for a firm to evaluate the impact of its new system.

....

....

d) Why do you think the cycle of change is described as **continuous**?

....

....

Q3 Explain what role **cost** plays in a company's decision on whether to make changes to its communication systems.

STAFF ANNOUNCEMENT: THIS IS OUR NEW, COST-EFFECTIVE COMMUNICATION SYSTEM.

....

....

....

Q4 Discuss the effects that a new and improved communication system might have on a firm's **employees**.

teleworking   redundant   re-trained   training   re-skilled   hot-desk   multi-tasking

The terms above might give you some ideas of what to write about in your answer.

No doubt your answer will be jam-packed full of ideas so it might be best to find yourself a piece of paper to scribble it on.

Section Six — Communication

How Businesses Use the Internet

Q1 Match each term on the left to the correct definition on the right.

- Internet — A piece of computer software which allows you to view websites
- World Wide Web — A huge collection of websites that can be viewed online
- Web browser — A network of computers covering the whole world

Q2 Which of the following statements are **true**?

a) Only very large businesses can afford to have their own website. ☐

b) Firms often use their websites to provide detailed information about their products or services. ☐

c) Most company websites are designed to be used mainly by a firm's employees. ☐

d) Firms can regularly update their websites to give customers up-to-date information. ☐

Q3 Suggest **three** ways a firm could use their website to provide customer services.

1. ....
....
2. ....
....
3. ....
....

Q4 The internet offers firms many opportunities for communication with their customers.

a) Explain the advantages of publishing a **product catalogue** on a website rather than printing it on paper.

....
....
....

b) Many firms include **guestbooks** and **online surveys** on their websites. Explain the benefits these can bring to the firm.

....
....

The mystery of the internet — it's a web of intrigue...
The internet has totally revolutionised the way firms work. If you'd said 20 years ago that in the future you'd be able to do your banking from home you'd have been put in the stocks and had rotten fruit thrown at you.

Business Websites — Benefits and Costs

Q1 Mandy wants to use advertising to increase the number of people visiting her business website. Suggest advantages that **internet adverts** may have for Mandy compared to other forms of advertising.

....

....

....

Q2 Many businesses now offer e-commerce facilities on their websites.

   a) What is meant by the term **e-commerce**?

   ....

   ....

   b) Explain how **consumers** can benefit from a business that offers e-commerce facilities.

....

....

Q3 Purrfect Catz Ltd. make cat accessories. They currently only sell their products in the UK. Explain how they could use the internet to expand their business.

....

....

....

....

Q4 Describe one way e-commerce can **reduce** business costs and one way it can lead to **increased** costs.

   Reduce costs: ....

   ....

   Increase costs: ....

   ....

Q5 Explain why it is important for businesses that sell online to make sure that their websites are secure.

....

....

....

Section Seven — Businesses and the Web

Domain Names and Hosting

Q1 Which of the following statements are true? Tick your answers.

a) A domain name is a way of identifying computers on the internet. ☐

b) One domain name is often used by several different websites. ☐

c) There are certain rules about how a domain name is constructed. ☐

d) Businesses have to keep paying a regular fee to carry on using a domain name. ☐

e) A domain name can also be called an IP address. ☐

Q2 Suggest **two** things a business should consider when choosing a domain name.

1. ....

2. ....

Q3 Explain the role of a **domain name registrar** in setting up a website.

....

....

Q4 Websites are hosted on servers.

a) Explain what is meant by the following **two** terms.

Web server: ....

Web host: ....

b) Suggest why a **small** firm is likely to use a web-hosting business to host their website.

....

....

c) Why might a large business use their own servers to host their website?

....

....

Q5 Some firms have websites that are not available on the internet.
Explain what these websites might be used for and how they might be hosted.

....

....

Spidey's favourite to win Wimbledon — he's a web server...

Don't worry, you don't need a deep technical understanding of how to host a website. You just need to know what these terms mean and how a business would go about getting its website online. Which is nice.

Section Seven — Businesses and the Web

Websites and the Law

Q1 How do data protection laws affect businesses that sell products or services online?

....

....

....

Q2 Websites must obey the Copyright, Designs and Patents Act 1989. How does this law affect a firm creating a website?

....

....

Q3 Any business that sells online must follow the same laws covering the supply of goods and services as High Street shops.

a) Describe three criteria that products must meet to comply with these laws.

1. ....

2. ....

3. ....

b) Explain why failing to obey these laws could be expensive for e-commerce businesses.

....

....

Q4 Selling goods online is a type of distance selling.

a) What is meant by **distance selling**?

....

b) There are laws covering distance selling which give consumers certain rights. What **three** main rights are given to customers by these laws?

1. ....

2. ....

3. ....

Don't violate copyright — that's patently obvious...

Wowsers. That page contained a whole lotta law. But chin up, you don't need to be a legal expert — just be familiar with the names of the relevant Acts, and be able to explain how they affect firms and their websites.

Section Seven — Businesses and the Web

Success of Business Websites

Q1 Businesses use many different methods to measure how successful their websites have been.

a) Explain how for some businesses, measuring the volume of calls to their customer telephone helpline can indicate how successful their website is.

....
....

b) How might this benefit the business?

....
....

Q2 Which **three** of the following do you think a business is **most likely** to use to measure how successful their website is? Tick your answers.

a) Counting the number of hits their website gets. ☐
b) Examining the results of surveys that customers have taken on their website. ☐
c) Seeing how often their website is mentioned in newspaper articles. ☐
d) Counting how many repeat visitors they get to their website. ☐
e) An email survey of customers to ask if they have access to the internet. ☐
f) A slightly creepy man holding a tape measure. ☐

Q3 FolderMart is a small business that sells office equipment. The firm sells its products through its shop, by mail-order catalogue and online through its website. In 2009 FolderMart launched a new version of its website. The graph below shows the firm's **overall** sales figures from 2008 and 2009.

a) The manager of Foldermart says,

> "The company's total sales figures have increased by £50,000 since the new website was launched. This proves that the website has been very successful."

Explain why Foldermart's overall sales figures **may not** be a reliable way to measure the success of its website.

....
....

b) Give **one** way a successful website may mean that FolderMart can reduce its costs.

....

Q4 Suggest why some businesses may choose to **not** have a website.

....
....
....

Section Seven — Businesses and the Web

Creating a Website

Q1 When planning a website, a firm will need to consider their budget they have to make the website.

a) Explain how a firm's budget can affect how their website looks.

....
....
....

b) Explain why a firm with a small budget may not offer e-commerce facilities on their website.

....
....
....

Q2 Explain why businesses need to consider the **equipment** that people might be using when they design a website.

....
....
....

Q3 When a firm has finished developing a website, it is rolled out.

a) What does it mean to 'roll out' a website?

....

b) Suggest why a website is **tested** before it is rolled out.

....
....

c) What **maintenance** does a website require after it has been rolled out?

....
....

Q4 The Chubby Goose is a restaurant on the English coast that attracts a lot of foreign tourists. The restaurant's owner has asked you to design a **webpage** displaying the restaurant's menu.

To answer this question, you'll need the file **ChubbyGoose**.
Flip to the inside front cover of this book for details of where to get it from.

The webpage should:
- have a **heading** containing the name and contact details of the restaurant
- display the **price** of each dish in **pounds**, **euros** and **dollars** (you'll have to do some research on the internet to find the current exchange rates)
- contain **hyperlinks** to Wikipedia articles where appropriate
- use a range of **text formatting** (font, size, highlighting etc.)
- be **designed appropriately** for the people you think are most likely to use the website

You can include any text, graphics or other features you feel would be suitable.

If you don't have access to web-authoring software, you can produce your webpage using a word processor, DTP or a graphics package.

Section Seven — Businesses and the Web

Section Eight — Business Applications

Word Processors: Text Formatting

> There's literally many practical questions in this section — all marked with this here symbol. Check out the inside front cover of the book for more info.

Q1 Open your word processor. Type the sentence below, and carry out the tasks described underneath.

> I'm such a lovely sentence, I couldn't possibly be improved.

a) Copy and paste the sentence three times.

b) Change the font formatting and colour...
   i) ...of the first copy to make it appeal to **children**.
   ii) ...of the second copy so that it would be suitable to put into a **formal business letter**.
   iii) ...of the third copy so that it looks like it could appear on the **movie poster** for an action film.

Q2 Below is a notice that a firm put up on their staff notice board. Read the notice and answer the questions that follow.

a) Describe **three** ways the formatting of the notice could be improved.

   1. ....
      ....
   2. ....
      ....
   3. ....
      ....

> Health and Safety Notice
> Staff are reminded that emergency exits must be kept clear at all times

b) Open your word processor and create a **new notice** with the changes that you have suggested. Use the information from the original notice — you don't need to change any of the words.

Q3 To complete this question, you'll need the file '**MarketingMemo**' (see the inside front cover for details of how to get it). The document contains information to be included in a memo to all senior managers at a firm. Make the changes below to complete the memo.

a) Increase the **font** size of the heading and **underline** it.

b) Insert **bullet points** in appropriate places. Indent these bullet points.

c) Put any job titles into **italics**.

d) Make **bold** any of the worker's names.

e) Change the **font type** and **colour** used to make it more appropriate for a **formal** memo.

f) Increase the **line** spacing.

g) Change the text so that it is **left-aligned**.

h) Explain how making all these changes will benefit the reader of the memo.

....
....

Word Processors: Text and Graphics

Q1 **Callouts** are used to label pictures and diagrams.
Open your word processor and complete the tasks below.

a) Find a picture of a **person** and insert it into your document.
Give the person a **speech bubble** and make them say hello.

It's best to use clip art here, 'cause it's illegal to get images off the internet without permission from the copyright holder.

b) Find a picture of a **clown** and insert it into your document.
Use **callouts** to label the following parts on your picture:

| red nose | big shoes | brightly coloured hair | garish clothes |

Q2 Below are two examples of how **text wrapping** can be used.
Use word-processing software to recreate these two examples.

No need to search high and low for a picture of a car exactly the same as this one. This is just a chance to practise a spot of text wrapping — so any old picture will do.

Q3 Most word processors allow you to play around with text and graphics on the page.

a) Why might you put text in a **text box**?

....

b) Why might you want to overlay text on graphics?

....

Q4 A take-away wants you to make a **flyer** which they can send out to advertise a new promotion.

a) What are the main features of a flyer which make it an appropriate way to advertise a promotion?

....

b) Open a new document in your word processor. Give it a suitable name and **save** it.

c) Insert a clip art picture of a pizza and make it the **background** to your document.

d) Give your pizza picture a **border**.

e) Use **WordArt** to give your flyer the title "Mario's Pizzas".

f) Explain why **WordArt** might be a better way to display the text on the flyer rather than ordinary text.

....

g) Use **WordArt** to put the words "Try our new 2 for 1 pizza promotion!" into the middle of the flyer.

h) Insert a **text box** at the bottom of your page and add the text
"Mario's Pizzas, Olive Street, Doughton. Tel: 09523 616 867".

i) Insert another **text box** and add the text "Open 7 days a week".
Move this text box around to decide where it will look best on your poster.

Section Eight — Business Applications

Word Processors: Text and Graphics

Q1 Hats All Folks Ltd. needs help organising some of their data, shown below.

a) Open a new document in your word processor. Give it a suitable name and **save** it.

b) Put the firm's data to the **right** into a **table** in your document.

c) The firm have decided to put some more information into the table. Add **two** extra rows to your table and put in the following information:

Year	Number of staff
2003	2
2009	33

Year	Number of staff
2004	2
2005	4
2006	6
2007	11
2008	15

d) What are the advantages of presenting data like this in a table?

....

Q2 The designers at Hats All Folks want some inspiration for their new designs. Complete the tasks below to put together some pictures for their use.

a) Open your **word processor**. Save your new document under a suitable name.

b) Give your document a **title** of "Types of hat" at the top of page.

c) Find **three** different clip art images of hats and **insert** each image into your document. Move the pictures round so that they all fit **neatly** onto the page.

d) **Label** each type of hat with its name.

Q3 Word processors allow you to put text in a document into **columns**.

a) Explain why text in documents like newspapers and newsletters is often put into columns.

....

b) Why is text in columns often **justified**?

....

c) Suggest **one** problem to look out for when justifying text.

....

Q4 Hats All Folks Ltd. need help putting together a newsletter. Open the file '**HatsAllFolks**' (see the inside front cover of this book to find out where you can get this file). This document contains all the text information they want to include in the newsletter. Below is a checklist of things the firm would like you to do.

- Make the newsletter's **title** more eye catching.
- Put the main body of text into **columns**.
- Insert your **data table** from Q1 into the appropriate place.
- Change the **font** size so the text fills the whole page
- Make any **subheadings** more eye-catching.
- **Justify** the text.
- Give the newsletter a **border**.

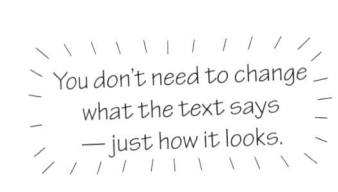

You don't need to change what the text says — just how it looks.

Section Eight — Business Applications

Word Processors: Business Letters

Q1 Many companies use a word processor's **templates** when writing their business letters.

a) What is meant by a template?

....

b) Give **two** reasons why a firm might use templates for their business letters.

1. ....

2. ....

Q2 Word processors allow headers and footers to be inserted into documents. What are headers and footers?

....

....

Q3 To the right is a letter which a firm sent out to one of its customers.

Label **three** features in the layout of this letter that are typical of a formal business letter. Number the features 2, 3 and 4 and describe what each feature is. The first one has been done for you.

1. *Date put at the top of the letter.*

2. ....

3. ....

4. ....

UK Mapz

UK Mapz
17 Contour Lane
Atlaston
MA1 2PS

October 12, 2009 ①

Mr Raleway
10 Comm Pass Way
Roadshire
LO1 2ST

Dear Mr Raleway

Thank you for your letter of August 25, 2009 informing us of a mistake on our Roadshire map. Here at UK Mapz we aim to produce the highest quality maps and are very sorry that our mistake led to you getting lost on your recent walk. We will be correcting our future maps. Please find enclosed a gift voucher to spend at your leisure on UK Mapz products.

Yours sincerely

Mr R Ivers
Manager Director of UK Mapz

There are definitely more than three things to pick here, so just pick the ones that jump out at you when you look at the letter.

Q4 Think of a company that you would like to work for. Write them a **formal business letter** asking if you could take part in a two-week work experience placement at their firm.

Your letter should include the following:
- fully-blocked **layout**
- formal **language**
- good **spelling**, **punctuation** and **grammar**

You could do an internet search to find the firm's address — you'll need to put this on your letter.

Your word-processor should have a letter template you can use.

Section Eight — Business Applications

Word Processors: Mail Merge

Q1 Most word-processors can produce a mail-merged letter.

a) What is meant by **mail merge**?

....

....

b) Explain how a business can benefit from using mail merge.

....

....

....

c) Explain **one** drawback of mail merge for each of the following.

Customers: ....

....

Businesses: ....

....

Q2 A firm wants to hold a meeting with its shareholders. They would like you to write a letter and perform a mail merge so they can send the same letter to each of their shareholders.

a) Open your word-processor. **Save** your new document under a suitable name.

b) Open the spreadsheet '**Shareholders**' — details of how to get this file are on the inside front cover.

Use the spreadsheet to create a **letter** inviting the shareholders for a meeting.
Your letter should contain the **merge fields** and **information** below.

Merge fields needed:
- Title
- Surname
- Address
- Town
- Postcode

Information needed in the letter:
- Name and address of the company: Plentiomonee PLC, 1 Factory Lane, Laborton, LB3 7GE
- The date of the meeting is 15th October 2009.
- The shareholders must arrive at 2pm at reception.
- The meeting will finish at 4pm.
- A map is enclosed to show them directions.
- The letter is from Mr W Orker, Chief Executive, Plentiomonee.

c) Perform the mail merge from part b). Preview each letter and make sure they're correct.

d) Explain why it is important to check your letters after a mail merge.

....

....

Learn how to make use of this e-merging technology...

Mail merge is one of those things you can read about until you're blue in the face but the best way to learn it is to practise it loads and loads. Keep trying it again and again until you can merge with your eyes shut.

Section Eight — Business Applications

Spreadsheets

Q1 To the right is a picture of a spreadsheet.

a) Which of the following statements about the coloured area is true?

i) The coloured cell's reference is 2B. ☐

ii) The coloured cell's reference is B2. ☐

b) What is the **difference** between a row and a column in a spreadsheet?

....

Q2 Most spreadsheet software allows users to change the formatting of their spreadsheets.

a) Suggest why you may want to change the formatting of a spreadsheet.

....
....

b) Explain what is meant by **conditional formatting**.

....
....

c) Suggest how **borders** might be used in a spreadsheet.

....

Q3 Enter the data below into a spreadsheet. Complete the following tasks to change the **formatting** of your spreadsheet.

Surname	First Name	Product bought	Price (£)	Amount owing (£)
Jones	Fred	Freedrop 2000	200	0
Ardman	Hyacinth	Curtains SL	150	0
Cleese	Wally	Nimbus 2006	300	12.56
Zooclutch	Marina	Contract 4	999.99	0.99

a) Make all the column headings **bold**.

b) Fill in any cell which contains a heading with a background **colour**.

c) Change the **width** of each column so that the data and headings fit.

d) **Insert** a column after "Product bought".
Give it the heading "Date bought" and input the following dates:
- Fred Jones bought his Freedrop 2000 on 16/11/2009
- Hyacinth Ardman bought her Curtains SL on 30/10/2009
- Wally Cleese bought his Nimbus 2006 on 06/11/2009
- Marina Zooclutch bought her Contract 4 on 02/11/2009

e) **Centre** the headings and text in the 'Price' and 'Amount owing' columns.

f) Use **conditional formatting** so that the numbers change colour if the customer owes money.

g) Select your table and **sort** the data so it appears in ascending numerical order by 'Date bought'.

Section Eight — Business Applications

Spreadsheets: Using Formulas

Q1 Nancy is the manager of a dry cleaning firm. She uses a spreadsheet to help keep records on the staff who work in the business.

a) Nancy wants to add up the data in column C of the spreadsheet to the right.

Suggest a **formula** she could use to add the data.

....

	A	B	C
1	Surname	First name	Hours worked per week
2	Goode	Phil	36
3	Slave	Lisa	40
4	Shirker	Kelly	24
5	Slouch	Peter	1
6	Total hours worked		

b) Nancy needs to work out how much to pay her workers.

	A	B	C	D	E
1	Surname	First name	Hours worked per week	Hourly wage	Gross wage
2	Goode	Phil	36	£6	
3	Slave	Lisa	40	£6	
4	Shirker	Kelly	24	£6	
5	Slouch	Peter	1	£6	
6	Total hours worked				

Gross wage just means the total wage before tax.

i) Write down the formula she should use in cell E2 to calculate Phil's gross wage.

....

ii) What would be the best way for Nancy to enter the same formula into the other cells in the column?

....

....

Q2 The formula =(B1+E3) is entered into cell **A1** of a spreadsheet. The formula is copied and pasted into each cell below. In each case, write down the two cells which will be referenced by the formula.

a) A4: .... and ....   b) E1: .... and ....

c) F9: .... and ....   d) J14: .... and ....

Q3 Nancy wants to increase the hourly wage of each of her workers.

Hint: keep the reference to the number of hours Phil has worked as a relative cell reference.

a) Recreate the spreadsheet from Q1 b), but **without the hourly wage column**.
 i) Pick an empty cell, any empty cell, and write £6 in it.
 ii) Change the formula for calculating Phil's gross wage so that it uses an **absolute** cell reference to your cell from part i).
 iii) **Copy and paste** the formula to calculate the gross wage of the other workers.

b) Change the hourly wage of each worker to £6.50 and write down each worker's new gross wage.

Phil: ....   Lisa: ....   Kelly: ....   Peter: ....

The formula for happiness =chocolatebiscuits+tea...

Formulas are fairly nice and easy to use. Absolute and relative cell references are a little bit trickier — know the difference between the two. Practise them loads and loads. Till you're absolutely sure how to do them.

Section Eight — Business Applications

Spreadsheets: Using Functions

Q1 To the right is part of a shop's spreadsheet showing sales of three products over a six-month period.

	A	B	C	D
1	Month	Tomato ketchup	English mustard	Cranberry sauce
2	July	89	72	3
3	August	92	65	6
4	September	56	32	8
5	October	45	17	14
6	November	61	20	45
7	December	34	16	102

a) Write down a **function** that could be used to find each of the following:

i) The **total** sales of ketchup during the six months.

....

ii) The **average** number of jars of English mustard sold in a month.

....

iii) The **maximum** number of jars of cranberry sauce sold in a month.

....

b) Suggest why it's often better to use a **colon** to define the range of cells in a function, rather than list each cell.

....

....

....

=SUM(all the gold)

Scrooge was a fan of functions

Q2 Below is part of a spreadsheet used by a car manufacturer. Open your spreadsheet software and recreate the spreadsheet.

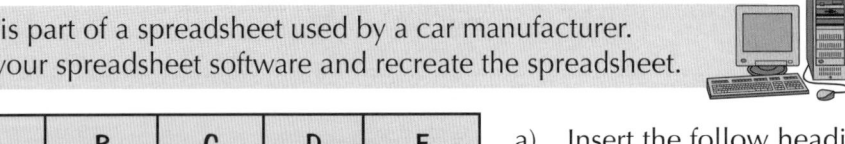

	A	B	C	D	E
1		Ignite Sportzy	Enviro Car V	Magna Car TA	Saloony
2	Monday	2	9	6	13
3	Tuesday	5	11	5	17
4	Wednesday	4	15	4	21
5	Thursday	6	12	3	13
6	Friday	4	8	6	15
7	Saturday	7	15	8	22
8	Sunday	2	7	1	13

a) Insert the follow headings in an appropriate place. You may need to insert extra rows or columns and merge cells.

i) Name of car

ii) Day of the week

b) Write down a function that could be used to work out the total number of Ignite Sportzy cars sold during the week.

....

c) Enter your function from part b) into the correct place on your spreadsheet. Copy and paste the function to find the total number of each car type sold that week.

d) The manufacturer aims to sell 35 of each car every week. Use the IF function to work out whether they have met their sales target for each car this week.

- If they have sold 35 or more of a car, make the word '**Yes**' appear.
- If they have sold fewer than 35 of a car, make the word '**No**' appear.

Section Eight — Business Applications

Spreadsheets: Graphs and Charts

Q1 Suggest when you might choose to use a **bar chart** to display data.

....

....

Q2 Graphs can be **edited** after they have been made. Suggest how you could edit a graph to make it easier to read.

....

....

....

Q3 Shopalotta is a chain of small supermarkets. Below is a spreadsheet containing data comparing the price of products sold in Shopalotta and three similar supermarkets.

a) Open your spreadsheet software and recreate the spreadsheet below.

	A	B	C	D	E	F
1				Name of supermarket		
2			Shopalotta	Pound-Or-Less	Savermans	SuperMK
3	Product	Milk (1 pint)	56	49	53	52
4		Small loaf	99	89	105	85
5		Tin of beans	95	30	62	35
6		Tomato soup	109	80	99	79
7		Custard creams	79	45	87	61

b) The director of Shopalotta wants to see some graphs comparing some of the data. Create the graphs listed below. For each graph you must include:

- a title
- labels for the axes
- a legend

i) A bar chart (column chart) to compare the price of each product at the four supermarkets.

ii) A bar chart (column chart) to compare the price of a tin of beans at all four supermarkets.

iii) A bar chart (column chart) to show the price of milk and tomato soup at Pound-Or-Less, Savermans and SuperMK.

c) Change the **colour** of the bars in your graph from part b) iii) so that the bars for tomato soup are **red** and the bars for milk are **white**.

Spreadsheets — not as comfortable as scatter cushions...

Aren't spreadsheets magical? You pop in your data, select a few cells, press a couple of buttons and ta da — you've got yourself a snazzy graph. Make your graph even more perfect by adding titles and labels too.

Section Eight — Business Applications

Spreadsheets: Graphs and Charts

Q1   Explain when it is appropriate to use each of the following types of chart.

Line graph: ....

....

Pie chart: ....

....

Q2   The tourist information offices in the seaside resorts of Sunnyville, Freesingleton and Chuckington counted the number of visitors to their offices between April and September 2009. Below is the data they collected.

	A	B	C	D	E
1			\multicolumn{3}{c}{Seaside resort}		
2			Sunnyville	Freesingleton	Chuckington
3	Month	April	235	231	187
4		May	182	156	163
5		June	267	284	205
6		July	364	452	267
7		August	489	501	321
8		September	291	256	178

Open your spreadsheet software and enter the data above.

a) Create each of the following graphs. For each graph you must include:

- a title
- labels for the x and y axes
- a legend

   i) Three line graphs (on the same axes) to show the number of visitors to the three tourist offices over the whole six-month period.

   ii) A line graph to compare the number of visitors to the Freesingleton and Chuckington offices in June, July and August.

b) The manager of the Sunnyville tourist information wants to see how the number of visitors to his office **each month** contributed to the total number of visitors to the office over the six months.

   i) Create a **pie chart** to show this information.

   ii) Give your pie chart a **title**.

   iii) Add **percentage** and **name** labels to each 'slice' of pie and then delete the **legend**.

   iv) Change the labels so that each 'slice' of pie is now labelled with the actual **number** of visitors each month, rather than percentages.

My pie charts are legendary — it's the way I bake 'em...

Once you've cracked making bar charts, there's nothing too different about making line graphs and pie charts. Just select the data you want to show and follow the instructions in your spreadsheet program. Just like that.

Section Eight — Business Applications

Databases

Q1 Databases store data in **tables**. These tables contain **fields** and **records**.

a) Explain the difference between fields and records.

....

....

....

b) Give three examples of **data types** that a field can contain. One has been done for you.

1. ......Text............................ 2. .... 3. ....

Q2 Below is a database containing information about the employees of a company.

First Name	Last Name	Job Title	Date of Birth	Employee No.
Ivor	Plane	Pilot	26/09/1964	75167
Lisa	Spanner	Engineer	01/12/1980	76432
Fred	Plane	Trainee Engineer	05/08/1987	79245
Holly	Sparrow	Pilot	25/12/1974	79429

See the inside front cover to find out where you can get this wonderful file.

a) Open the database '**EmployeeData**' and make the following changes:

   i) Holly is now married. Her new surname is 'Copter'.
   ii) Fred has left the company. **Delete** his record from the database.
   iii) **Add** the details of these new employees:
   - Malcolm Function, Accountant. Date of birth: 14th March 1969. Employee number: 79621
   - Liz Leader, Marketing Director. Date of birth: 20th October 1977. Employee number: 79643
   iv) **Add** a new field with the field name 'Gender', whose entries will be either "M" or "F". Enter data in this new field to record whether each employee is male or female.

b) Explain what is meant by a **key field** in a database.

....

c) Which field in the database above would be the best choice for the **key field**, and why?

....

Q3 Databases can be either **flat-file** or **relational**.

Your answer to part a) should mention tables and key fields.

a) Explain the difference between a flat-file database and a relational database.

....

....

b) Give one advantage of using a relational database rather than a flat-file database.

....

....

Section Eight — Business Applications

Databases: Data Input Forms

Q1 **Data input forms** can be used to enter data into a database **table**.

a) Explain why it's important for data input forms to be designed in a clear and logical way.

....

....

b) What is an **input mask**?

....

c) Why might it be useful to **display** any input masks that have been used on a data input form?

....

....

Q2 Read the information below and complete the tasks that follow.

> Ryan runs a gig venue. He wants to gather information on the people who use the venue and their music tastes so he can inform them about gigs that may be of interest to them.

a) Create a **database table** with the fields listed below.
   Select an appropriate **data type** for each field.

   | ID | First Name | Surname | Address | Postcode | Date of Birth | Favourite Music |

   Set "ID" as your key field.

b) Ryan wants to give the customers three options for their favourite type of music — **pop**, **rock** or **disco**. Create a **drop down menu** for the Favourite Music field so that only these three options can be selected.

   Hint: You'll probably need to change the data type for this field so you can create the menu.

c) Create a **data input form** that Ryan could use to enter his customers' details into the table.

   Hint: If your database program has a wizard, that's the easiest way to do this.

d) Below is some data that Ryan has already collected by hand.
   Enter this information using your data input form.

   > Justin Timberine, 5 Riverside Lane, CR8 2YM, 13/05/1982, pop
   > Calvin Harrison, 28 Discot Road, RF2 8TW, 18/06/1984, rock
   > Oscar Osbawn, 8 Rockcliffe Avenue, BA5 9TS, 28/03/1963, rock
   > Kylie Minogle, 33 Lucky Lane, LO3 9CO, 18/09/1974, pop
   > Kenny East, 13 Rappin Close, BL6 3NG, 27/01/1967, disco

   Check that your data has been inputted correctly into your table.

I love a good database — that's my input on the matter...

In your exam you might be expected to design and create your own data capture form. Eek. Just make sure you're happy with how to link the text boxes in your data input form to your database table and you'll be fine.

Section Eight — Business Applications

Databases: Simple Queries and Sorting

Q1 What is the difference between **sorting** and **filtering** data in a database?

....

....

Q2 Match the following types of search with the correct symbol.

- a) Finds values equal to a certain amount
- b) Finds values less than the amount specified
- c) Finds values not equal to the amount specified
- d) Finds values greater than or equal to the amount specified

- i) <>
- ii) >=
- iii) <
- iv) =

Q3 Wildcard searches are a useful technique to use with databases.

a) Explain what is meant by a **wildcard** search. Which symbol would you use to perform one?

....

....

b) Describe what would be found if the following wildcard search criteria were used in a text field.

i) Like "A*" ....

ii) Like "*my" ....

iii) Like "P*s" ....

Q4 Twinton College keeps a database of all the students who have signed up to its ICT evening class. Open the file '**TwintonCollegeData**' (see the inside front cover of this book to find out where to get it).

a) **Sort** the records so that they are in ascending alphabetical order by surname.

b) Use queries to **search** the database to find the records of the following people. Sort your results in ascending order of ID.

   i) Students with the surname "Taylor".

   ii) Students from the town of Twinton.

   iii) Students whose first names start with the letter J.

   iv) Students whose title is not "Ms".

   v) Students with the surname "Brown" who have paid.

   vi) New students whose surnames start with the letter P.

Section Eight — Business Applications

Databases: Simple Queries and Sorting

Q1 The customer records from a trouser manufacturer are shown in the database below.

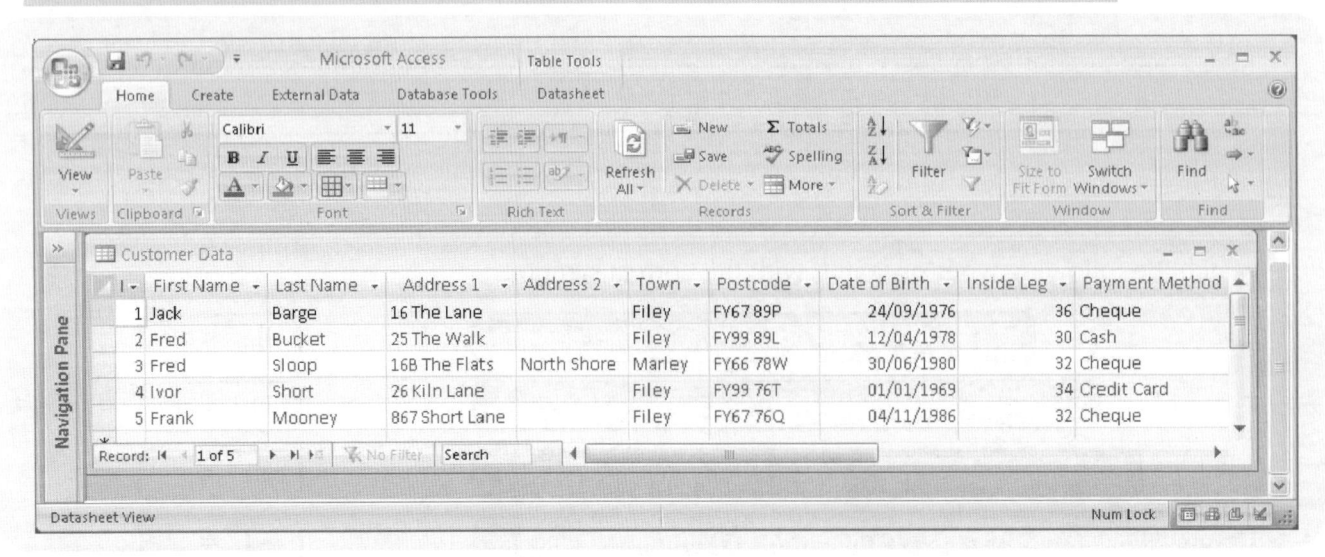

I	First Name	Last Name	Address 1	Address 2	Town	Postcode	Date of Birth	Inside Leg	Payment Method
1	Jack	Barge	16 The Lane		Filey	FY67 89P	24/09/1976	36	Cheque
2	Fred	Bucket	25 The Walk		Filey	FY99 89L	12/04/1978	30	Cash
3	Fred	Sloop	16B The Flats	North Shore	Marley	FY66 78W	30/06/1980	32	Cheque
4	Ivor	Short	26 Kiln Lane		Filey	FY99 76T	01/01/1969	34	Credit Card
5	Frank	Mooney	867 Short Lane		Filey	FY67 76Q	04/11/1986	32	Cheque

State which **person** (or **people**) would be found by each of the four queries below.

a) Criteria: Inside Leg = 30

This query would find: ....

b) Criteria: First Name = "Fred", Town = "Filey"

This query would find: ....

c) Criteria: Date of Birth < #01/01/1970#

This query would find: ....

d) Criteria: Town = Not "Marley", Payment Method = "Cheque"

This query would find: ....

Know how to put data into order? Guess you're sorted...

And you probably thought that once data was in a database there was no more fun to be had — but you can merrily sort and search to your heart's content. Know how to uses quotes, symbols etc. in your queries too.

Section Eight — Business Applications

Databases: Producing Reports

Q1 Database software allows you to produce **reports**.

a) Which of the following can be used as the data source for a report? Tick the correct box(es).

☐ a table ☐ a form ☐ a query

b) Explain why reports are often a better way to display database information than the data table itself.

....

....

c) Database software usually allows you to add **headers** and **footers** to a report. Explain why these might be useful on a really long report.

Hint: Headers and footers work the same way in database reports as they do in word processors.

....

....

> For the next few questions, you'll need the files '**TwintonCollegeData**' and '**TwintonCollegeLetter**' — see the inside front cover of this book to find out where to get them.
> The database contains details of people who have signed up for an ICT evening class at the college.

Q2 The course administrator wants to find the details of any students who aren't from the local area.

a) Design a query to find the names and home town of students who **don't live in Twinton**.
- The search results should display these fields only: Title, First Name, Surname and Town.
- The results should be sorted in ascending alphabetical order by surname.

b) Use a **Report Wizard** to produce a report to display this information. Give your report a **title**, and make sure the **field names** are clearly displayed.

Q3 The course administrator also wants to find which of the local students are **new to the college**, and what their **ages** are.

a) Design a query to find out the names and dates of birth of the **new students from Twinton**.
- Your results should display these fields only: Title, First Name, Surname and Date of Birth.
- The results should be sorted in descending order by date of birth.

b) Produce a **report** showing this information. But this time, design your own report **from scratch**. Give your report a different layout and colour scheme to the one you made in Q2.

Q4 The finance department at Twinton College wants to send reminder letters to all the students who haven't yet paid the tuition fee for the ICT course.

a) Design a query to find the full names and addresses of anyone who **hasn't yet paid** the college.

b) Open the file '**TwintonCollegeLetter**'.

Use this template and your search results to perform a **mail merge** to create reminder letters that can be sent to the people whose payment is overdue.

Section Eight — Business Applications

Graphics: Creating Images

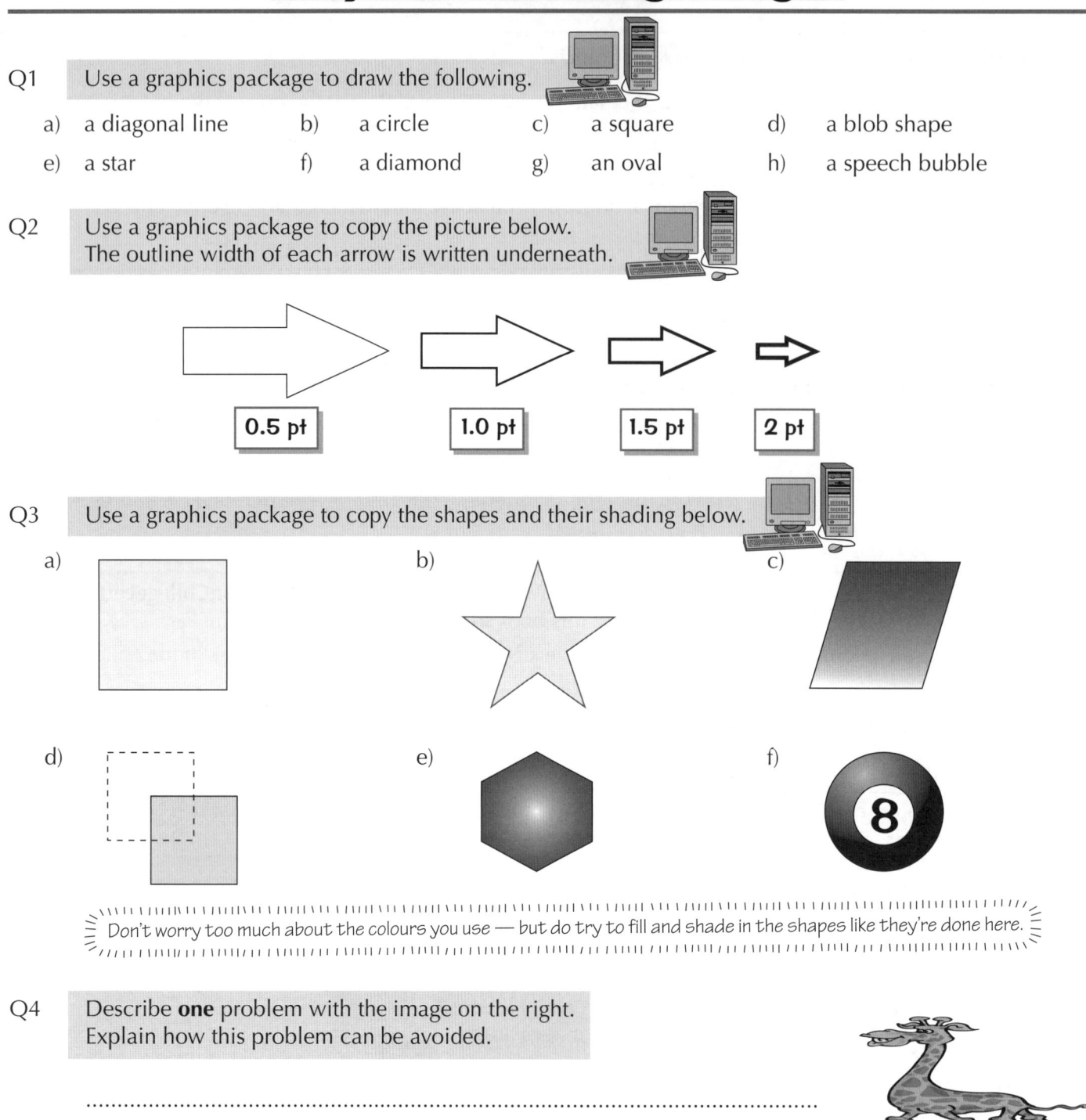

Q1 Use a graphics package to draw the following.

a) a diagonal line   b) a circle   c) a square   d) a blob shape

e) a star   f) a diamond   g) an oval   h) a speech bubble

Q2 Use a graphics package to copy the picture below.
The outline width of each arrow is written underneath.

0.5 pt   1.0 pt   1.5 pt   2 pt

Q3 Use a graphics package to copy the shapes and their shading below.

a) b) c)

d) e) f)

Don't worry too much about the colours you use — but do try to fill and shade in the shapes like they're done here.

Q4 Describe **one** problem with the image on the right.
Explain how this problem can be avoided.

....

....

....

Q5 A graphics package can be used to edit existing images.
Open a graphics package and complete the tasks below.

a) Find a clip art picture of a cat and put a top hat on him.

b) Find a clip art picture of a man and replace his head with a robot's head.

Creating images — it's a shady business...

You might be able to do these graphics in your sleep but have a go still — it's fun to do things you're good at. I'm really good at writing funny little bits to fill these boxes up. All up. Right to the end. With funny little bits.

Section Eight — Business Applications

Graphics: Manipulating Images

Q1 Images can be **cropped** using a graphics package.

a) What does cropping mean?

....

....

b) Draw **lines** to show how you could crop the picture to the right so that you are left with **only the moon** in a square shape. The first line has been done for you.

c) We've provided some images to help you with the following tasks. (Take a look at the inside front cover to find out where to get these.)

   i) Open the image '**Book**'.
      Crop the image so you are only left with the book.

   ii) Open the image '**HandsomeMan**'.
       Crop the image so you are only left with a picture of the man's head.
       Marvel at his tremendous beauty and thoughtful expression.

   iii) Open the image '**Boats**'. Crop the image so you are only left with a picture of the boats.

Q2 Describe **two** ways an image made in a graphics package can be put into a word-processor document.

1. ....

2. ....

Q3 Complete the following tasks below to insert a picture into a word-processor document.

a) Open the image '**Fireworks**' (see the inside front cover to find out where you can get this image). **Crop** the image so you are only left with a picture of the fireworks and **save** it under the name 'FireworkDisplay'.

b) Open up a new **word-processor document**.
   Add the title "Bonfire night extravaganza".

For some extra word processor practice, why not turn this into a flyer for a bonfire night display?

c) Put your picture into the document using **one** of the two methods in Q2.

d) Move the picture around until you are happy with its position.

e) Save your word document and print it.

f) Take it home and stick it on your fridge.

Q4 Suggest why someone might choose to use word-processing software to make a graphic, rather than use a graphics package.

....

....

Section Eight — Business Applications

Presentation Software

Q1 A manager at a firm is planning to give a presentation to his employees.

a) Describe the **main features** of each of his presentation options below:

Slideshows: ....

Flipcharts: ....

OHTs: ....

b) Why is **visual** communication important in a presentation?

....

....

c) The manager has decided to create a slideshow using presentation software.
Why might he choose to use **animation effects** in his presentation?

....

Q2 The Managing Director of Cheez Factory Ltd. is giving a presentation to some new employees. Use presentation software to complete the tasks below to create a **slideshow** to accompany his speech.

a) On the first slide:
  i) Add the text "An Introduction to Cheez Factory Ltd."
  ii) Change the **colour** and **size** of this text until you are happy with it.

b) Add another slide.
  i) Give it the title "Cheez Factory — a brief history".
  ii) Add the information below. Use bullet points and animations.

> Cheez Factory Ltd. founded in 1984. 34 different types of cheese. 200 employees. Distribute to all the big name supermarkets. Profits of £5.2m last year.

c) Add another slide.
  i) Give it the title "What next for Cheez Factory?"
  ii) Insert a **picture** of a piece of cheese onto your slide, no bigger than half the slide.
  iii) Add a **text box** and insert the text "Organic cheeses". Draw a line from the box to the picture.

d) Change the **background** colour of all your slides to blue and **save** the presentation.

Q3 The Managing Director of Cheez Factory Ltd. would now like to use the presentation with some other staff. Open up a new slideshow and complete the tasks below.

- On the first slide insert the title "Cheez Factory — a recap".
- Insert slides 2 and 3 from the 'Introduction' slideshow.
- Make the picture of the cheese on slide 3 **bigger**.
- Add a **transition** between all the slides.

Section Eight — Business Applications

Presentations

Q1 To the right is a slide that was used in a company presentation. Suggest **two** ways in which the appearance of the information included in the slide could be **improved**.

1. ....

2. ....

> **How did we do last year?**
> Compared with last year (2008) our profits were up by 2.3%. Making 2009 our most successful year since the firm began in 1987. We opened up our new factory in Chorley, increasing the number of people that work for the company to 2,300. We also increased the number of products that we sell and stopped production of some products where sales were greatly reduced. We launched our new website to help increase our e-commerce. It was a great success as our online orders increased by 300%. The new website is much easier to navigate and has much more information available. We have decided that after the success of the website we will no longer produce our catalogue three times a year, but reduce this to once a year. It'll be released in October ready for the Christmas period. We have high hopes that sales from our website will increase so much that we will eventually reduce the number of shops we have, and reduce some costs this way. Last year also saw the retirement of our longest serving member of staff, Joe Young. He'd been with the company since 1987 and had helped us become the great company that we are today. He hopes to play lots of golf in his retirement and take lots of well earned holidays.

Q2 Give **two** disadvantages of using electronic presentations over other forms of visual presentation.

1. ....

2. ....

Q3 The manager of a marketing team is holding a meeting with his team of three staff to discuss ideas about a new project.

a) Explain why the manager might decide to use a flipchart to show information in the meeting, rather than a slideshow.

....

....

b) The manager must now present the ideas from the marketing meeting to a group of 30 people from different departments in the firm. Explain why he might now choose to use a slideshow to present the information.

....

....

Q4 You have been asked to give a talk describing your favourite TV programme or film. You must use a slideshow presentation as part of your speech. It should be **four** slides long.

a) Open up a **new** slideshow and save it under a suitable name.

b) Make your presentation and include the following features:

| transitions | animation effects | background colour | graphics |

c) Add **notes** to each of your slides for you to use in your presentation.

d) Print off **one** copy of your presentation with your notes on.

e) Print off **one** copy of your presentation with all **four slides** on the same page.

Animation effects — I cried at that film with the deer...

In an exam you might be asked which presentation techniques are appropriate for different situations — so be familiar with the benefits and drawbacks of each. And know how to make your slideshows eye-catchingly brill.

Section Eight — Business Applications

Web-Authoring Software

Q1 Explain why a firm's website should have a **consistent** page format and layout.

....

....

....

Q2 Describe the **purpose** of each of the following features on a web page:

Frames: ....

....

Hyperlinks: ....

....

Borders and lines: ....

....

Q3 Give **one** benefit and **one** drawback of using high-resolution images on a website.

Benefit: ....

Drawback: ....

Q4 Using suitable software, create a website about a holiday destination.

Your website should be made up of at least **three** web pages and should include the following:

- A front page briefly **describing** the holiday destination.
- A page describing **things to do** in your chosen holiday destination.
- A page describing **places to stay** in your chosen holiday destination.

This could be anywhere — you could pick somewhere you'd really like to go.

It should also have the following features:

- different font sizes
- different font colours
- different font types
- hyperlinks to all your pages
- coloured backgrounds
- borders
- images

These are all the sorts of things an examiner might want you to include on a web page.

Don't feed sweets to a lynx — it makes them hyper...

Making web pages isn't too different from making slideshows. It's fairly easy to get good marks for making a web page — have a go at all the things mentioned above and make your pages consistent in style. Tidy.

Section Eight — Business Applications

Other Software Applications

Q1 Describe the **similarities** and **differences** between a word processor and a desktop publishing package.

....

....

....

Q2 Most email software allows users to create **address books**.
Explain one way in which this feature might be useful to a business.

....

....

Q3 Some firms use **diary-management** software.

a) Describe **two** uses of diary-management software.

1. ....

2. ....

b) Suggest **one** way in which using diary-management software could benefit a firm.

....

....

Dairy-management software is less useful.

Q4 How does **project-planning** software allow firms to manage projects more efficiently?

....

....

....

Q5 Blogs and Wikis are two examples of **Web 2.0** websites.

a) Explain what is meant by a Web 2.0 website.

....

....

b) Suggest **two** ways a business could benefit from writing a blog.

1. ....

2. ....

c) Why might an online wiki encyclopaedia be less reliable than a well-known printed encyclopaedia?

....

Section Eight — Business Applications

Evaluating Software

Q1 Suzie works for a company that sells package holidays. She is using a **word processor** to produce a newsletter that will be sent to the firm's customers.

a) Suzie wants to make a picture of a boat to put into the newsletter. Explain why using the word processor's **drawing tools** may not be the best way for Suzie to produce this picture.

....

....

b) Explain why a **graphics package** would be a better method of producing the picture.

....

....

Q2 Most businesses need to store and process **financial** data. Explain why many businesses use **spreadsheets** to do this.

....

....

....

Q3 For some packages, users can choose between **proprietary** software and **open-source** software.

a) Give **one** difference between these two types of software.

....

b) Toby is an IT expert. He works as a sole trader, designing websites for local business. Toby has decided to use an open-source web authoring package for his work. Suggest **two** possible reasons for this decision.

1. ....

2. ....

Q4 **Web-based software** is accessed through the internet rather than being installed on the user's computer.

a) A hospital is considering changing the database package it uses to store its patients' medical records. Explain **one** reason why a web-based package might not be suitable in this situation.

....

....

b) In some large businesses, people working on the same project may be located in different places. Explain **one** benefit that web-based software could have for this kind of team.

....

....

Section Eight — Business Applications

Assessment Skills
79

Controlled Assessment

If you're taking the AQA or OCR exams, your controlled assessment will involve studying the media and methods of communication that businesses use. This might include analysing a <u>website</u>.

The questions on this page are all based on the web page below — you'll need a separate sheet of paper to answer some of them.

Q1 The boxes below contain some of the features that businesses often include on their websites. Tick all the features you can see, and draw arrows pointing to **one** example of each of these on the page.

Logo ☑   Company name ☐   Slogan ☐   Strap line ☐   Images ☐

Contact details ☐   Graphs and charts ☐

Menus ☐   Hyperlinks ☐

Navigation buttons ☐   Prices ☐

Visitor counter ☐   Enquiry forms ☐

Clear space ☐   Bullet points ☐

Filmic Cinema, Pinkington - Internet browser
http://www.filmiccinema.co.uk/

Filmic Cinema
Bringing you the best in film since 1953
Address: Barnaby Street, Pinkington, Leicestershire, Pl3 8NN   Tel: 05351 785932

Home | **Films now showing**
Now showing
Coming soon — **Springy and Leo (U)**
Book tickets   Mon–Sun 11.00am, 2.00pm, 4.30pm
Kids' club   Springy the kangaroo has his world turned upside-down when he's thrown out of his marsupial tribe for a crime he didn't commit. Left to wander the streets of Sydney alone, he meets Leo — a streetwise city cat with a heart of gold. Together they form an unlikely team to prove Springy's innocence.
Special offers
How to find us
FAQs   Heart-warming animal comedy fun for all the family. Click here for more information.
Competitions
Useful links   **The Day of Bad Things (15)**
               Mon–Sun 3.00pm, 7.15pm, 9.45pm
               Dave Oakbough is an ex-Marine, haunted by his troubled past. Now working as a reporter for the Los Angeles Gazette, Dave discovers a criminal plot to kidnap Hollywood actors and hold them to ransom. When the police refuse to believe his story, he's forced to take on the plotters single-handed.
               High-octane action thriller featuring cameo

Films now showing
• Springy and Leo (U)
• The Day of Bad Things (15)
• Supercrazy (12)
• Eleanor's Question (12A)

Films coming soon
• James and the Clockwork Trolls (PG)
• Duet of Death (15)
• Signs of Wear (12A)

Kids' Club Films
Weekdays at 11.30am

Q2 Now look more closely at the cinema's **logo**.

a) Which words best describe the **image** this logo gives of the business? You can tick more than one box, and suggest your own words.

Fashionable ☐   Traditional ☐   .... ☐
High-tech ☐   Knowledgeable ☐   .... ☐

b) Explain how the design of the logo helps to put this image across.

Q3 The web page includes a box that advertises Kids' Club Films — it uses two different **fonts**. What image do you think each font creates? Explain your answers.

Kids' Club Films
Weekdays at 11.30am

Q4 Now look at some **real** business web pages and analyse them in the same way as you did in Q1–3.

Obviously the <u>content</u> of every web page will be different, but you can still use the same <u>techniques</u>. Start by noting down all the <u>features</u> that are used on the page. Then look at some of them in more detail — what <u>message</u> are they conveying, and <u>how</u>?

Analysing website features — it's a feature-length task...

The questions on this page have picked out a few website features to get you started. When you're analysing a real web page, think about <u>all</u> the features in Q1 — what are they <u>for</u>, and <u>how well</u> do they <u>work</u>?

Assessment Skills

80

Controlled Assessment

> The flyer below has been made by a business who offer maths tuition to school students. They have printed 10,000 copies which will be delivered to housing estates near schools in the local area.

Q1 Read through the flyer and then answer these questions.

a) What **message** is the business trying to communicate?

b) Which group of **people** is the flyer aimed at?

c) What is the business hoping these people will **do** when they've received the message?

Takeaway Maths

Proffesional tuition that makes maths as easy as $x, y, z!$ ✓

Are your kids finding maths a struggle?

Let's face it — not everybody is a big fan of maths. Its easy to get stuck on a tricky concept like trigonometry or calculus and loose your confidence.

At Takeaway Maths, we understand this. That's why all our maths tutors are patient and sympathetic with kids of all ages — from Key Stage 1 right up to A-Level. We're so confident in our methods, we guarantee that your child's grades will improve after only four weeks of tuition!

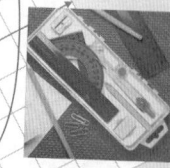

Takeaway Maths founder Chris Jennings spent ten years as a teacher before remortgaging his house to gain the start-up capital he needed to set up the business.

I studied non-linear dynamical systems at university, so I know my stuff when it comes to maths — and so do all of Takeaway's tutors. Our relaxed style makes maths fun. Call or visit our website today!

www.takeawaymaths.com   Tel: 03432 9583771

"Maths is rubbish."

Q2 Think about the places the flyer will be **delivered** to (see the box at the top of the page).

a) Based on your answers to Q1, do you think a flyer was a good choice of **medium**? Explain your answer.

b) Suggest **other media** the business could also use to get their message across. Explain your suggestions.

Q3 The flyer uses **written communication**.

a) Find examples of each of the following in the flyer:

    technical jargon   irrelevant information

    spelling/punctuation errors

    statements that might be exaggerated or untrue

b) For each of the features you found in part a), explain the **effect** they have on the message overall.

Q4 Discuss how effectively the flyer uses **visual communication**.

> E.g. how much do the photos add to the message? Is there any 'visual noise' that makes the message harder to read?

Q5 Businesses need to make sure all their communications create the right **image**.

a) Use two or three words to describe the **overall image** you think the flyer creates of the business.

> There's no 'right' answer here. Here are some suggestions: businesslike, friendly, honest, reliable, smug, educational...

b) What image do you think the business was **trying** to create? Again, just use two or three words. Are these the same words as you used in part a)?

Q6 Think about your answers to Q3–Q5. Suggest **improvements** to the flyer that would help to solve the problems you identified in these questions.

> Aim to make sure that your improved flyer would clearly deliver the message and image that the business wants to put across.

Q7 Repeat questions 1-6 with some **real** business documents.

> You don't have to use flyers. Have a look at websites, adverts, catalogues... whatever you can get your hands on.

Assessment Skills

Exam Marks

Marking other people's exam answers can help you see how easy it is to lose marks if you're not really careful. So have a look at the answers on these pages and be ready to play the part of an examiner...

Q1 Below are two students' answers (and marks) for the following question.

> Explain what is meant by 'teleconferencing'. (2 marks)

> Teleconferencing is when a meeting is held using a telecommunications device — for example, a video screen or a telephone line. ①
> **Anita**

> Teleconferencing uses communication technology (such as a telephone line or a video link) to allow people in different locations to have meetings. ②
> **Rachel**

Why do you think Rachel was awarded more marks than Anita?

....

....

Q2 Read Jo's answer to the exam question below and answer the questions that follow.

> Using an example, explain what is meant by 'remote data storage'. (2 marks)

> If a business stores all of its data on its own premises, it could lose a lot of information if the building is burgled or damaged in a fire. Remote data storage involves keeping data on a different site so that it can be retrieved even if the main office burns down. For example, web-based storage services can be used to keep data on internet servers. Or data can be saved to magnetic tape in a different building. ②

a) Cross out anything you think could be removed from Jo's answer without affecting the mark.

b) Jo said later that: "It's best to write loads for each question, because that way you're bound to say the right thing eventually." Why might Jo's strategy not be the best way to approach an exam?

....

Q3 Below is an exam question and its mark scheme, along with Gethin's answer.

> DoublePlus Finance is a business that offers financial advice. A manager at the company is considering the most suitable way to store customers' data.
>
> Explain one disadvantage to DoublePlus Finance of using portable storage devices. (2 marks)

> Portable storage devices can be lost or stolen. They can also be used to transmit viruses from one computer to another.

Mark Scheme	Description of answer	Marks
	No valid response.	0
	The answer **identifies** a disadvantage.	1
	The answer **applies** the disadvantage to the case study.	2

Use the mark scheme to mark Gethin's answer. Explain why you have given him the mark you have.

This answer gets ..... mark(s) out of 2 because ....

....

Assessment Skills

Exam Marks

Writing long answers to essay-style questions is tricky. Marking them isn't the easiest thing in the world either, as you're about to find out. There are two mark schemes this time — and you need to use both.

Q1 Below is an exam question and Ellen's answer.

> Horsley's Bank is a banking business with around 20,000 customers. Every month it sends each customer a statement in the post to show the money that has gone into and come out of their account.

i) The managers of Horsley's are considering scrapping these paper statements and making the data available on a secure website with password protection. Do you think this would be a good strategy? Explain your answer. (10 marks)

> Sending statements by post costs Horsley's money on paper, printing and postage — the bank could reduce these costs by switching to a website. There would still be costs involved in setting up and maintaining the website, but in the long term it would probably be cheaper than sending out thousands of letters each month.
>
> It is also important for the data in the statements to be kept secure, since they contain customers' private financial details. Paper statements are not ideal, since they can be lost or stolen from the ordinary post. It is more difficult to steal data from a password-protected website, but Horsley's would need to invest money in a high level of online security to prevent the data being seen by unauthorised users.
>
> Some customers may not have access to the internet, or may feel uncomfortable about viewing confidential information online. However, many other customers will prefer the convenience of the website, since it can be viewed at any time, not just once a month. As more and more people in the UK gain access to the internet, Horsley's will need to invest in online services to stay competitive.
>
> Overall, I would say that replacing paper statements with a website is a good strategy for Horsley's. Ideally, they should give their customers the choice of whether to receive their statements by post or on a website.

This first mark scheme is used to assess a student's Business and Communications knowledge, and their understanding of the scenario in the question.

Mark Scheme 1

Description of answer	Marks
No valid response.	0
The answer **identifies** strengths and weaknesses of each medium.	1–2
The answer **applies** these strengths and weaknesses to the case study.	3–4

a) Use the mark scheme to mark Ellen's answer. Explain why you have given her this mark.

This answer gets .... mark(s) out of 4 because ....

....

This second mark scheme is used to assess a student's ability to analyse and evaluate evidence. It's also where you get marks for the "quality of written communication".

Mark Scheme 2

Description of Answer	Marks
The answer gives a judgement with **some** support and justification. Ideas are communicated with some **structure** and occasional use of **technical terms**.	1–3
Candidate offers judgement with **justification**. Ideas are communicated with a **clear structure** and correct use of some **technical terms**.	4–6

b) Re-read Ellen's answer. This time use this second mark scheme to give her a mark out of 6. Explain why you've given her this mark.

This answer gets .... mark(s) out of 6 because ....

....

Assessment Skills

Sample Exam Questions

1   Read **Source 1** below and then answer the questions that follow.

> **Source 1**
> Reyah is a manager at a company that designs and makes toys and games. Her team works closely together on design projects. The whole team currently works in an open-plan office, and each member of staff works from 9 a.m. until 5.30 p.m. Monday to Friday.

(a) What is meant by an 'open-plan office'?
(1 marks)

(b) Explain **one** advantage to Reyah's team of working in an open-plan office.
(2 marks)

(c) Reyah is considering introducing flexitime and teleworking to her team.

   (i) Explain what is meant by 'flexitime'.
   (2 marks)

   (ii) Explain what is meant by 'teleworking'.
   (2 marks)

(d) Would you recommend introducing flexitime and teleworking to Reyah's team? Explain your answer.
(6 marks)

2   Read **Source 2** below and then answer the questions that follow.

> **Source 2**
> Chris runs a mail order company that sells customised T-shirts. At present, they send a catalogue to customers on their mailing list and take orders by post or telephone. This information is then entered into a database by the company's staff.

(a) State **two** input devices that could be used to enter data into the database. Explain what each device might be used for.
(4 marks)

(b) Chris wants to allow their customers to enter their own details using a data input form on their website. Explain **two** advantages this could have for the company.
(6 marks)

(c) Chris realises that it is important to keep customers' personal data secure.

   Identify and explain **two** types of software Chris could use to protect data from unauthorised users.
   (6 marks)

Assessment Skills

3   Read **Source 3** below and then answer the questions that follow.

Source 3

Linda is a manager at *Amazoglaze*, a business that sells double-glazed windows. Many of its sales are made by staff who telephone potential customers or call at their houses.

Linda wants to recruit a new salesperson to her team. She has produced a job description that outlines the main duties involved in the job, and a person specification that describes the qualities that the ideal candidate would have.

(a) The new salesperson will be paid a basic salary plus commission.

   (i) Explain what is meant by 'salary'.
   (2 marks)

   (ii) Explain **one** reason why Linda might choose to pay her staff a low basic salary with high rates of commission.
   (3 marks)

(b) Linda asks all applicants for the job to send a CV and a completed application form.

   (i) Describe the main features of these two documents.
   (4 marks)

   (ii) Explain how Linda could use these documents to create a short-list of candidates.
   (2 marks)

(c) Explain **one** reason why Linda would want to interview short-listed candidates before offering them a job.
   (3 marks)

4   Read **Source 4** below and then answer the questions that follow.

Source 4

Mahir is a manager at a company that makes and sells home electrical equipment such as vacuum cleaners, microwaves and food blenders. The business currently sells its products in well-known shops and provides customer support through a telephone helpline.

(a) Mahir wants to launch a company website that would include e-commerce facilities.

   (i) Explain what is meant by 'e-commerce'.
   (1 mark)

   (ii) Explain one benefit that e-commerce can have for customers.
   (2 marks)

(b) Explain **two** disadvantages that having a website may bring to the business.
   (5 marks)

(c) As part of the website's services, Mahir plans to offer customer support by email. Customers will be able to send questions through the website and receive a written response by email. Evaluate the use of email rather than a telephone line to provide customer services.
   (9 marks)

Assessment Skills